Making the
Ordinary School Special

Tony Dessent

Area Educational Psychologist
Cambridge County Council-Education Authority

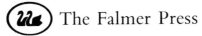 The Falmer Press

(A Member of the Taylor & Francis Group)
London, New York and Philadelphia

UK   The Falmer Press, Falmer House, Barcombe, Lewes, East Sussex, BN8 5DL

USA   The Falmer Press, Taylor & Francis Inc., 242 Cherry Street, Philadelphia, PA 19106-1906

First published 1988.   Reprinted 1988, 1991.

Library of Congress Cataloging in Publication Data

Dessent, Tony.
  Making the ordinary school special.

  Bibliography: p.
  Includes index.
  1. Handicapped children—Education—Great Britain.
2. Mainstreaming in education—Great Britain.   I. Title.
LC4036.G7D47   1987   371.9′046   87-9010
ISBN 1-85000-235-5
ISBN 1-85000-236-3 (pbk.)

Jacket design by Caroline Archer

Typeset in 11/13 Bembo by
Imago Publishing Ltd, Thame, Oxon

Printed in Great Britain by Burgess Science Press, Basingstoke on paper which has a specified pH value on final paper manufacture of not less than 7.5 and is therefore 'acid free'.

Contents

Acknowledgements

The ideas expressed in this book have evolved from my work with children, parents, teachers, psychologists and others, too numerous to name, in Cambridgeshire and elsewhere.

I would like to acknowledge Cambridgeshire County Council for seconding me to pursue a year's study and research at the University of London Institute of Education during which time this book was written. I am grateful to Norman Coulson (Cambridgeshire's Principal Educational Psychologist and Senior Inspector for Special Education) and to Professor Klaus Wedell at the London Institute of Education for their guidance and support, and to Phil Ellender for his meticulous reading of the initial draft of the manuscript. Last, but not least, my special thanks go to my wife Suzanne and my children, Mandy and Chris, for their tolerance before, during and after the writing of this book.

Foreword

It is four years since the 1981 Act on Special Educational Needs came into force, but the full implications of the way in which it defined 'needs' are only gradually beginning to be fully recognised. The definition indicates that special educational needs have to be explained in terms of the interaction between features of the child and of the environment; that the degree of need is judged in relation to expectation and that the dividing line between ordinary and special provision is determined by how far a Local Education Authority makes its primary and secondary schools comprehensive. This book offers a detailed analysis of what it means to face up to these implications.

During a year's study, based at the University of London Institute of Education, Tony Dessent visited and met with a wide range of people, throughout the country, to find out about their ideas and about the directions in which their thinking was turning with regard to meeting special educational needs. In this book, he examines existing policies and practices, and considers the principles which should guide future development. The book does not make comfortable reading, because it shows that many of our present assumptions need to be questioned. Just because of this, however, it is essential reading for all those with responsibilities in this aspect of education. Readers will have different views about Tony Dessent's proposals, but whatever their conclusions they, just as I, will have benefited from having tested their views against his challenge.

Klavs Wedell
Professor of Educational Psychology
(Children with Special Needs)
University of London Institute of Education.

Chapter 1

Introduction

Ordinary schools can become special. This book is concerned with the practical steps that need to be taken if ordinary schools are to meet the special educational needs of children. It is a book about both 'special' education and 'ordinary' education. The view taken is that by becoming special, ordinary primary and secondary schools can extend the idea of comprehensive education to include those children presently excluded from the mainstream educational system. Moreover, by becoming special, ordinary schools can move closer to meeting the individual needs of *all* children.

The merger of special education with mainstream education presents an enormous challenge for all concerned. There is, nevertheless, reason for optimism. Concepts of special education, both in Great Britain and elsewhere, are rapidly changing and evolving. We now better understand what special education is, who needs it and why. This conceptual revolution in our understanding of special education is occurring at the same time that searching and fundamental questions are being asked within our society about the nature and aims of education for all pupils — special or otherwise. Obstacles to change do exist. However, central to this book is the view that, within the context of evolving concepts and fundamental questioning, there exists the potential for creative policy making. Such policies could enable 'ordinary schools to become special' and in so doing blur, our largely arbitrary distinction, between the 'ordinary' and the 'special' child.

To realize the potential for change requires an understanding of the obstacles which exist. Within the field of special educational needs the obstacles to change towards a less segregated system are considerable. Despite the influence of a comprehensive national report on special educational needs (DES, 1978), the subsequent government legislation (DES, 1981) and major LEA-based reports such as that of the Fish Committee (ILEA, 1985a), large numbers of children with special needs are still being 'streamed' out of mainstream primary and secondary schools. Educational sociologists have, in recent years, begun to draw attention to the possibility that the 1981 Act and the 'new' concept of 'special educational needs' could result in more, rather than fewer, children being provided for in some form of segregated educational provision (Tomlinson, 1982). In 1985 Will Swann, from the Open University, asked the question, 'Is the integration of children with special needs happening?'. His answer, based upon an analysis of DES statistics of the numbers of children attending separate special schools from 1978 to 1982, was that, 'Overall, there is no evidence of a trend towards integration ... in the case of children with learning difficulties and those termed maladjusted there is clear evidence of a trend towards increasing segregation, especially in the primary age group' (Swann, 1985).

Why has a system of segregated special education continued to survive in spite of the various legislative, professional and parental pressures for a more integrated system?

What are the obstacles confronting schools, teachers, parents, support services and LEA policy-makers in this area?

Is the only problem the absence or lack of resources?

Are teachers in mainstream schools ill-equipped or unwilling to provide for the needs of handicapped and disadvantaged children?

Is the issue really to do with the absence of any coherent LEA policies linked to the integration issue?

Does the continuation and maintenance of a segregated special educational system reflect wider, social and cultural views concerning the nature and purposes of schooling, and the place within it of those with so-called 'special needs'?

These are some of the questions addressed in this book. As the factors which both facilitate and hinder the goal of making ordinary schools special are considered, a view will be put forward concerning the changes which need to occur and the action which needs to be taken in order to reach this goal.

Scope and Emphasis

Special education — what it is, where it occurs, and how — is not the concern of any one group, in or outside of education. Special education is a part of the wider education system. Its existence is also intimately related to questions of public and professional values and attitudes; to questions of financial resources and costs; to questions concerning teaching, teachers and the nature of schools and schooling in our society. When considering the theme *Making The Ordinary School Special* three levels of analysis can be discerned (see table 1). In recent years, the social, political and economic context of special education (Level 1) has received increasing attention (for example, Barton and Tomlinson, 1981 and 1984; Tomlinson, 1982). In addition, a number of researchers have documented those aspects of school-based policies (Level 3) which facilitate, or impede, the greater involvement of children with special educational needs within mainstream education (for example, Galloway, 1985; Reynolds, 1976; Rutter *et al,* 1979).

Table 1: Making The Ordinary School Special

Level 1-Social, Political and Economic Context
For example, the aims of the education system and the place of 'special' children within it;
public and political attitudes towards education and 'the handicapped';
how much should be spent on the handicapped?

Level 2-LEA Policies
For example, finance and resourcing;
administrative and advisory structures;
role of support services;
policy on integration/segregation.

Level 3 School-Based Policies
For example, 'Whole school' approaches;
curriculum and teaching methods;
school organization, school ethos and the 'hidden curriculum'.

Aspects of LEA policy (Level 2) have, however, received relatively scant attention, even though most researchers, practitioners, teachers and parents recognize the crucial influence of LEA-based policies. The particular policies and direction taken by each LEA will determine the kind of educational provision which might be on offer to an individual child with special needs. LEA policies also exert a massive influence via their capacity to facilitate *in school* policy and provision (Level 3) for all children who may experience educational difficulties. This book will be concerned with all three levels of analysis. However, particular attention will be directed towards the area of LEA policy and service organization and to the development of whole-school policies for children with special needs. Emphasis too, will be placed upon the majority 'group of children' with educational difficulties — those children with learning and social/behavioural problems. This group forms over 80 per cent of both the total population of special schools and units (DES, 1982) and of those children in mainstream schools considered by teachers to have special needs (Croll and Moses,

1985). It would appear that, in comparison with this majority group, the needs of children with sensory and physical handicaps are more readily met within mainstream schools (Swann, 1985). Teachers would seem to be much less threatened by the presence of an obviously handicapped child in a mainstream classroom (Dessent, 1983), and there is clear research evidence of more favourable attitudes towards the integration of such children amongst mainstream primary teachers (Croll and Moses, 1985). The major challenge to the development of non-segregated educational provision is posed by children with moderate learning difficulties and a range of social behavioural problems.

'Non-segregation' Versus Integration

Many of the research studies which have been carried out in Great Britain concerning children with special needs, have been related to the issue of integration. The focus has been upon particular integration projects — usually attempts by LEAs and schools to provide, within mainstream settings, for a group of special needs children who might formerly have attended a special school (for example, Hegarty, Pocklington and Lucas, 1981; Hegarty, Pocklington and Lucas, 1982). Such studies, however, leave untouched the central issue of how an individual child or group of children comes to be regarded and labelled as having special needs in the first place. The term 'integration' carries with it the implication that the children exist first as a segregated group — different from and unlike their 'normal' peers. This segregated group then require, or can be offered, 'integration'. While at a common sense level we can recognize that certain groups of handicapped or disabled children are clearly different, and therefore 'special' in some way, this is by no means the case with the great majority of children with special educational needs — those with learning and social difficulties. The concern of this book is less with the *integration* of children who have historically been provided with some form of separate special education. The focus instead, will be on the issue of *non-segregation*, and upon 'extending the concept of normality' within mainstream education (Jones, 1985). By developing non-segregation policies the need for the segregaton of particular groups of children should be minimized. Such policies would also reduce the need for LEAs to 'statement' individual pupils and then make 'special' provision for them. A concern with non-segregation must be closely linked with the concern for a fully comprehensive education system. Non-segregation policies at both national, LEA and school level, will involve consideration of organizational, resourcing, training and curriculum processes which broaden the acceptable range of normality of ordinary schools. As a result, both obviously handicapped children and the majority group of educationally disadvantaged children, should be better provided for in the main-stream system. An over-emphasis on the notion of integration can divert attention from the issue of non-segregation, since it carries an inherent notion of initial segregation. Central to the idea of non-segregation is the concept of a continuum of special educational needs.

The Continuum of Need

The notion of special needs as forming a continuum is both uncon-troversial and readily understood. The implications of the concept are, however, quite revolutionary when the business of resource allocation and the organization of special needs provision is considered.

Historically, special education has operated on what might variously be described as a 'handicapped', 'medical' or 'diagnostic' model. Whatever the term used, the common feature was the use of a 'within child' explanation of special educational needs. Children, in these models, are seen as *possessing* a handicap, a learning difficulty, 'ESN(m)ness', emotional disturbance etc. Of course, the 10-handicap category approach of the 1944 Act was consistent with this notion. Both the legislation and the concepts of special need which under-pinned it fitted neatly into the idea of separate special educational facilities. The logic being that children 'ascertained' as ESN(m) needed, of course, ESN(m) education (within or outside of ordinary schools).

The model carried with it several other ideas which have mas-sively influenced the way in which special education has developed within local education authorities in Great Britain. Firstly, 'special education' became synonymous with the child who attended a special school or special unit. Other children, who remained in mainstream classes, required a different terminology — 'remedial', 'slow learning', or (indicating a 'near miss') 'borderline special school'. The system spawned the idea of a 'special school child', a phrase still frequently used amongst mainstream, special school and support service staff. The assumption was that there was a *sharp divide* between children who required special education and those that did not. Moreover, that there was a *finite number* of the former requiring only the highly specialised skills of the 'ascertainers' (psychologists and doctors) to reveal who they were. A further notion which developed as part of this model was that 'special school children' required something quite different in terms of their educational diet than did other children. Thus, the myth that there existed a distinctive form of expertize in special education began to develop (see chapter 6).

Now it is easy to regard such a model as historical (if not archaic) and hopelessly inadequate for the way in which special needs are currently perceived. However, it was a model which governed our approach to special needs for some forty years, and aspects of the model had relevance for *some* children. This is particularly true if we consider the needs of the most profoundly physically, mentally and sensory handicapped children. For such children the 'within-child' notion might be seen as largely appropriate. The numbers of such children are relatively small and, at a common sense level, there does appear to be clear differences between the needs which arise from their disabilities and the needs of other 'normal' children. Even with children with such profound difficulties the 'within-child' model of the 1944 Act had limitations. A sympathetic and modified learning environment is capable of minimizing the effects of most disabilities. Indeed, an appropriately modified environment could overcome the handicapping effect of a disability in a particular situation. However, the problem, historically has been that a model which had, at least, some relevance for a small minority of children has been used to develop our approach for all children with special needs.

Warnock's concept of special educational needs as forming a continuum, and embracing the legendary '20 per cent' of children considered to have special educational needs (DES, 1978), accelerated the lengthy and continuing process of changing our whole way of thinking about special education. Figure 1 represents a model of the continuum of special needs. The continuum is a continuum of need rather than a continuum of ability or disability. It relates to the need which any individual child may be seen to have for assistance, support and intervention, in order to pursue an educational programme. At the far right of the continuum are the children who require a considerable degree of help and support in their learning. They are likely to be the children with the most serious disabilities and handicaps in our communities. They are small in number and for administrative purposes are readily countable. At the far left of the continuum are those children who experience some kind of moderate difficulty in any area of learning, social adjustment or physical development. Such pupils require less extensive and less intensive forms of assistance in order to support their learning. Numbers can

Figure 1: The Continuum of Special Needs

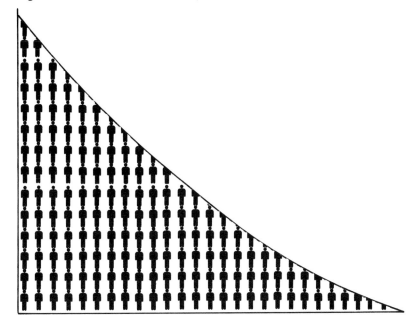

Numbers of Children with Special Needs

Increasing Level of Need

be large in this group although the overall number of children across the continuum depends totally, and crucially, upon particular learning contexts and expectations. The notion that up to 20 per cent of the school population have special education needs is now a familiar one. However, the idea of a child 'having a special need' makes little sense outside of particular learning contexts. If the learning environment is 'sympathetic' and geared towards meeting individual needs, there will be few special educational needs. The continuum of need must, therefore, always be seen within this relative context.

'Special education' — its provisions, resources, administrative and advisory structures — exists somewhere along the continuum. The most important feature of this model of need is that *there is no break in the continuum*. If an individual child is picked out from the continuum as being, in some sense, deserving of particular special attention in terms of, say specialist teaching, individualized help / additional staffing, there will always be a child, not so regarded, who is only marginally dissimilar in terms of need. Educational psychologists, who have, in recent educational history, been key figures in defining special needs, are very familiar with this ethical and professional dilemma. Teachers too will frequently be aware that other pupils in their class sometimes differ in only a small degree from a pupil who is 'referred' and (in the language of the current legislation) 'formally assessed' as being in need of special education. Wherever a line is drawn through the continuum of need (for example, for the administrative purpose of allocating resources, the production of statements etc.) it will always be an arbitrary one. Neither educational psychologists nor any other educational or medical specialist possesses tests or criteria which can discern a special educational need from a non-special educational need which is able to stand any close scrutiny. Similarly, many teachers in mainstream schools when discussing special needs will comment that 'all children have special needs'. Thus, while it may be possible to agree upon the relative extent of each individual pupil's needs for extra attention and care, and to place these along some kind of continuum — decisions concerning *who* has and *who does not* have a special need are fraught with problems. Such decisions are also subject to variations between teachers, schools and local education authorities. It is not surprising therefore that there exists a huge overlap between the needs of children who have traditionally been placed in special schools and those that have remained in mainstream education. Nor is it surprising to find that the proportion of children placed in separate special schools varies enormously between LEAs. In 1985 the percentage of the school age population placed in separate special schools or units of some kind in England ranged from .9 of 1 per cent, in one LEA, to 5 per cent in another.

What is a Special Educational Need?

'Special education' and 'special educational needs' can only be defined relative to 'ordinary' education and relative to what we understand as being, the ordinary needs of children. 'Special education' is a term which describes those forms of educational provisions which are not considered 'normal' or 'ordinary'. Using the terms of the current legislation, special education is educational provision which is not made 'generally available'. In the same way, a 'special educational need' can only be defined in terms of needs which are 'ordinarily' or 'normally' met. All children have educational needs. If the educational needs of an individual child are not met by the processes of 'ordinary' education, then that child might be regarded as having a 'special educational need'. What this implies is that, ultimately, the term 'special' could be dropped from our educational vocabulary. If more and more of the needs which we now call 'special' are met by the ordinary processes of education, fewer special educational needs will exist.

The problem of determining and defining a special need is further complicated by the clear and gathering evidence that both home and school factors can exacerbate and can themselves create special educational needs (Galloway, 1985; Rutter *et al*, 1979; Reynolds, 1976 and 1982). Such evidence further points the way towards both an interactive and a relativistic concept of special educational needs. Wedell (1983) comments, 'the problems of the handicapped are the result of the *interaction* between the nature of their deficiencies, and the nature of their environment. The needs of the handicapped are, therefore, seen to be relative *both* to the deficiencies "within" the child *and* to the deficiencies of the environment'. Special educational needs can be regarded as existing only within some kind of context of 'expectations of normality'. Wedell (1981) notes, 'the term "special educational need" refers to the gap between a child's level of behaviour and achievement and what is required of him'. The ultimate relativistic view might be that — 'many children have special needs because what they are asked to do is too difficult for them!'

Interactive/relativistic concepts of special needs and the notion of an unbroken continuum of need pose enormous ethical and practical problems for politicians, administrators, support services and schools themselves. Who is special and who is normal? Who should receive additional 'special' resources? Who should receive the 'protection' of a statement under the terms of the 1981 Education Act? Which children are 'resource worthy' and which not? Who should decide, and what criteria should be used? Much of the controversy which currently surrounds discussion of special educational needs relates to these questions. The ten categories of handicap listed in the 1944 Act and the myth that there existed a finite group of 'special school children' have, in the past, provided relatively comfortable administrative answers to such questions. The great challenge for special education in the future will be the development of non-segregation policies. Such policies should enlarge the concept of comprehensive education by matching the range of educational provision to the full range of educational need, without loss to the rights and dignity of the most handicapped and vulnerable children in our schools. In the process, administrators and policy makers will need to look at issues well beyond those concerning the needs of individual pupils. Current concepts of special needs are increasingly pushing special education into areas such as school ethos, school organization and curriculum reform and, at the broadest level, into a consideration of the politics and aims of education as a whole.

Chapter 2

Meeting Special Needs in Ordinary Schools — A Question of Values

What would a mainstream school, which was providing for *all* children with special needs in its community, look like? How attractive would such a school be to parents living in the area which it served? Can ordinary schools afford to be special in the sense of providing for all children with special educational needs? In attempting to answer these questions, it is possible to gain some insight into the social, economic and political issues which relate to the development of non-segregation policies. These issues will be the focus of concern in this chapter. The links between special education and public and political values concerning the nature and purposes of education will be examined. The view taken here is that any analysis of special educational needs must begin within the context of what education as a whole is seen to be about.

Let us return to the notion of an idealized, fully comprehensive school. Further, let us view the school from the perspective of a group of visiting parents of prospective first year children. Their purpose is to make a choice about their child's future secondary school placement. Now parents as a group will vary in terms of the criteria by which they may make judgments about the quality and desirable attributes of a school. However, it is likely that a substantial majority will value highly schools which emphasize a disciplined and orderly educational environment, respect for the teacher's authority, teacher directed learning and, in particular, schools which can declare a high level of success in public examinations. It would be naive to denigrate such values as being ill-informed or 'conservative' since they probably represent the dominant value system of parents in Great Britain at the present time. Interestingly, when it comes to considering their own children's secondary education, such values often seem to guide the thinking of many teachers, advisers and academics who expound more radical views about the aims of education! What would this imaginary group of parents see as being offered to pupils in this fully comprehensive school? What would the curriculum look like? How would pupils and teachers interrelate? Would formal or informal forms of dress and address be in evidence? Most importantly, for the current analysis, would the parents like and value what they see and make that school their choice on secondary transfer? The suggestion here is that such a school, in its attempt to meet the needs of a wide range of children with special needs (particularly those who have been regarded as disaffected, disruptive or maladjusted), would need to make radical changes in its ethos, rule structure, curriculum and teacher-pupil relationships. The result could be that the school would present as an unattractive choice for this intending group of parents. It might be predicted, for instance, that a substantial number of the school's less academic pupils would be engaged in a range of practical and recreational curriculum activities which bore little resemblance to traditionally held notions of 'education'. Informal dress amongst pupils and informal forms of address between pupils and staff are likely to feature, at least amongst older pupils. A consistent emphasis in the curriculum might be on pupil directed, rather than teacher directed activities. Such a school is likely to have abandoned rigid forms of grouping by ability and to have de-emphasized the usefulness of public examinations in guiding their curricula. Whether such changes in school organization, ethos, curriculum and teaching methods are a *necessary part* of meeting the full range of special needs is not known since it is very unlikely that any secondary school in Great Britain has ever fully developed such a philosophy. It is, however, likely that meeting children's special needs within an integrated mainstream context will have widespread implications for all aspects of schooling. There are likely to be implications for *all* pupils, including the academically and intellectually most able.

If this speculative example has validity, then it might be concluded that the views held by the majority of parents concerning education and the nature and purposes of schooling may not be consistent with meeting a wider range of special educational needs within ordinary schools. The concern here, of course, is with the broad social, political and economic context within which special education functions. Educational sociologists have in recent years increasingly focussed attention upon the nature and purposes of special education and, in particular, on the idea that special education serves particular 'social interests' within society (Barton and Tomlinson, 1984). Such writers stress the view that special education, while construed on the one hand as 'doing good' to children within a humanitarian framework, works at another level as a form of social control. Thus, the smooth running of a normal education system is seen as depending in large measure on the removal of 'misfits' and potentially troublesome groups of children via special education. Such children are seen as representing a potential threat to those aims and goals of schools concerned with the maintenance of discipline, control and the pursuance of academic excellence and examination credentials for the academically successful. Thus, special education is seen as primarily serving the interests of the school system rather than the individual pupils. Barton and Tomlinson (1984) go further in suggesting that special education in advanced technological societies —

> ... is now a more important mechanism than it has ever been for differentiating between children, and allocating some to a lifestyle that — if not as stigmatized as in the past — will almost certainly be characterized by dependence and powerlessness. In addition, the economic recession in these societies has bought into sharper focus a perennial question in special education — 'How much should be spent on groups who may not be economically profitable or useful in the society?'

Within this latter context it is possible to view the operation of the 1981 Education Act, particularly its requirement for formal, multidisciplinary assessment and 'statementing', as a means of controlling and delimiting public expenditure. This system had its origins in the Warnock Committee's humanitarian desire to protect and safeguard the interests of children with severe, complex and long-term disabilities. LEAs talk now about the 'protection of a statement'. However, the assessment and statementing process is lengthy, bureaucratic and consumes considerable amounts of professional time from teachers, psychologists, doctors and administrators. It acts effectively as a 'funnel', its very processes restricting the numbers of children who receive 'resources additional to or otherwise' not available in normal schools' (DES, 1983). Statements can be seen as operating a dual form of 'protection'. The protection, as Warnock intended, of resources for a small minority of those children with severe and complex special needs, but *protection also for LEAs from providing additional resources for the larger numbers of children with special needs.*

The sociological analysis of special education appears sometimes to be over-stated (see Croll and Moses, 1985). It seems to rest unduly on the notion that there is an 'enemy in the system'. It is possible, for instance, to view the development of special education not as a device to 'remove the misfits', but as part of a genuine attempt to serve the interests of individual handicapped pupils. The approach, in illuminating aspects of social control and the vested interests which are within special education, usually fails to distinguish between the effects of and motivation for actions taken by individuals. This point is well made by Lindsay (1985) ... 'It is one thing to point out to those involved in the system, and parents and children themselves, that their actions do not lead to the ends they (or others) desire. It is quite another thing to attribute self-interest as being the professionals' main motivation.' The sociological analysis does, however, provide some essential insight into the way in which special education functions within the context of the educational system as a whole and its social, economic and political functions. It highlights the very real obstacles relating to values and attitudes, both political and public, which hinder the development of non-segregation policies for children with special needs.

'There are No Votes in Children with Special Needs'

Special education has traditionally been a relatively low status area of the educational system. It has been a 'fringe area' activity — a field which has rarely come to the forefront of educational debate, either within education itself or amongst the general public. It has sometimes been seen as an area of refuge for teachers who have 'struggled to cope' and make career progress in the mainstream sector. Its low status has been reflected in the level of responsibility bestowed on both administrative and advisory officers within LEAs and upon 're-medial' and special needs teachers within schools. 'Remedial education' has traditionally been the first area to be 'cut' when educational economies have to be made (Lukes, 1981). The lowly status of remedial and special education is, as we have seen, intimately related to widely held values concerning the aims and purposes of education. As Booth (1983) comments,

> Discrimination against handicapped people is a consequence of a system of values which rewards and applauds people for their talents and physique. It is revealed by the fears of mothers that they may give birth to a handicapped baby and by parental aspirations for their children. It is enshrined in an educational system which progressively excludes children on the grounds of their ability.

Schools themselves are subjected to powerful social pressures to ensure that they place academic achievement and examination success — as opposed to providing for the needs of the less able — high on their agenda. Such pressures come in an explicit form from parents and in more subtle forms from LEAs (elected members, administrative and advisory officers). LEAs typically monitor their schools' performance in terms of examination successes. The question could be asked as to whether advisers and administrators sometimes develop their 'picture' of the overall state of health of a secondary school in terms only of the number of passes achieved by pupils in public examinations. Certainly, few LEAs have established systems of monitoring schools in terms of other 'success' factors such as levels of attendance and truancy — nor indeed of less easily measurable variables, such as the level of disaffection amongst pupils, the relevance of curricula to children's perceived needs, etc. The important point about these inherent values is not that they are misguided, but that they are most likely to represent our *own* values for our *own* children.

The implications of such values are profound when it comes to considering the way in which resources are distributed disproportionately within the educational system. The social and political pressures on schools inevitably lead to, often unquestioned, allocations of financial resources (teacher time and teacher expertise) towards the *most able* rather than the least able children in schools. The smallest teaching groups in many secondary schools, often taught by the 'best' qualified teachers, are to be found in sixth-form teaching groups. LEA administrators and advisers are familiar too with what might be termed 'resource drift'. This occurs when teaching or financial resources accorded to schools because of the needs of handicapped or less able children — drift over time to other areas of the school's work which are perceived as having a higher priority. Take, for instance, the case of a secondary school which is provided with some additional teacher time in order to meet the school's 'special needs'. The headteacher could decide, however, that the greatest need in the school is for an additional teacher to bolster science teaching for examination classes. The resource may then be used in this area rather than to enhance provision for children with educational difficulties. Similarly, within primary schools, teachers themselves and LEA support staff are aware of the oft criticized practice of some headteachers of using remedial or special needs staff to 'cover' for absent/sick teaching colleagues. Thus, resources which have been specifically earmarked for low status special needs are often diverted and redirected unless 'protected' in some way within the 'market place' of the ordinary school system.

Practices such as these indicate perhaps an underlying value system which upholds the view that priority for resources in the educational system should go to the potential wealth providers (academically able pupils), rather than to pupils who are seen as contributing little to the future economic prosperity of the nation. Arguably, what we have, in mainstream education, is a system of positive discrimination for the most able pupils in our schools.

The issues being discussed here are essentially ethical in nature. Indeed, any discussion of special education is unavoidably a discussion concerning questions of value and ethics in terms of the distribution of society's educational resources. Putting aside the powerful pressures on schools concerning examination success and individual achievement, *every classroom teacher,* whether in a primary or secondary school, faces and resolves, each day, decisions concerning the distribution of their own time resources. The research of Croll and Moses (1985) indicates that, within mainstream primary school classrooms, children with learning and behavioural difficulties consume more of a teacher's individual time and attention than those pupils regarded as not having special educational needs. Yet, such disproportionate allocations of teacher time can be problematic. Any teacher could quite justifiably maintain that, 'all children have special needs'. The implication being, perhaps, that all children have an equal right to the teacher's time and expertise and that no one child has a right to a disproportionate amount. Related to this issue is the fear sometimes expressed by parents in schools where an integrated 'special' unit or facility is developed that, 'the ordinary children will suffer or lose out in some way because of the attention being given to children with special needs'. Similarly, discussion with mainstream teachers concerning children with special needs rarely avoids teachers raising the question, 'What about the gifted?'. Teachers are often anxious to point out that children, at both ends of the ability range, might be seen as having a special need, and therefore to be equally deserving of special attention, or, in the terms being discussed here, a disproportionate slice of the school's resources. What these foregoing examples have in common is the difficulty of justifying, at the level of schools and individual classrooms, a decision to allocate a disproportionate amount of teaching and financial resources to any one group of children. *What is absent, in most ordinary primary and secondary schools, is an agreed and uniformly applied principle of positive discrimination towards children with special educational needs.* Instead a separate special educational system has been used to resolve the ethical problems in deciding 'resource worthiness'.

A Policy of Positive Discrimination

Policies concerning positive discrimination in the distribution of re-sources to disadvantaged groups are neither new nor unusual. The Plowden Report's recommendation that schools in socially disadvan-taged areas should receive enhanced resourcing is one example from recent educational history (DES, 1967). Home Office policies relating to ethnic minority needs provide a current example of positive discri-mination measures (Local Government Act, 1966). Interestingly, spe-cial education is rarely conceptualised in this way. Yet it is clearly the case that the various provisions and resources (special schools, units, advisory, peripatetic and support staff) which constitute an LEA's special educational system represents just such a policy. Special schools and units are usually more favourably staffed and resourced at all levels than are mainstream schools (see chapter 5 for a fuller discussion of resourcing policies). In evolving a pattern of special educational provision, a system has been constructed which effectively legislates for a positive discrimination principle for children with special needs. The current system has a number of characteristics. Firstly, it partially removes many of the ethical decisions regarding the distribution of resources from the shoulders of mainstream schools, LEA advisers, administrators and elected representatives. It provides a formalized and regulated system of dealing with the ethics of 'resourceworthiness'. Headteachers can, when confronting the pressures produced on staff and other children of a particular indi-vidual pupil's needs — 'refer' such a pupil for consideration for extra resources to this separate system. This avoids the need to consider any further redeployment of the school's own resources for the individual child in question. Should a decision be reached by an LEA, (usually via the procedures of the 1981 Act) that the child should receive additional teaching/non-teaching help in the ordinary school, then this *disproportionate allocation of resources* has been *legitimized* by factors outside of the school. Headteacher and teaching staff are no longer in a position of needing to justify a policy of positive discrimination for this individual child. The decision has been taken by others and they are effectively (and arguably, quite reasonably) 'off the ethical hook'. Ordinary schools which have pupils with 'statements' on roll will often comment that meeting these pupils' needs is considerably easier than meeting the needs of marginally dissimilar pupils who do not have statements. The suggestion here is that this occurs not solely because of the additional resources which schools may accrue. Of equal importance is the fact that complex moral and ethical issues concerning resource distribution have been partially removed from the arena of the school. Thus, support service personnel will frequently find that, even when schools are provided with adequate 'special' resources, there may still be a perceived need for agencies outside of the school itself to define who should be in receipt of those resources and who should not.

A second, and related, characteristic of our special educational system is that of its separateness from the mainstream. Special education resources come from a different budget heading and are often managed and distributed by a separate group of LEA officers. Its separateness is related to the perceived need to 'protect' resources for children with special needs over time. The issue of protection is a central one to be grappled with in any consideration of developing special needs provision in mainstream schools. A view frequently taken is that resources allocated to children with special needs in mainstream schools, are subject to cuts, changes over time and misuse unless protected in some way. A phrase used by one LEA officer when discussing the use of statements was that they protected children from 'accidental neglect' on the part of LEAs. What a separate special education system is seen to do is to remove the issue of positive discrimination in the use of resources for children with special needs from other competing areas and interest groups. It seems likely that the rapid expansion of the special school system since the 1944 Act, was closely related to the fact that a separate system provides a neat and tidy administrative solution to the problem of protection and positive discrimination for children with special needs. The more favourable resourcing which pupils in special schools receive is legitimized by the formal processes of ascertainment. Further, the management responsibility for justifying and deploying additional resources to such pupils is removed from the 'sight and minds' of ordinary schools. The perceived advantages of such a system bring in their wake major problems when considering the development of non-segregation policies. The system encourages the identification and processing of *individual pupils* as being special and thereby picks them out from the continuum of special need. A corollary of protection is often segregation; the segregation of teaching facilities, the segregation of 'special' staff and the segregation of feelings of professional and personal responsibility for children with special needs. The principle of positive discrimination which exists in traditional special education systems has many strengths, but seems to be an unsatisfactory one when considering ways of helping ordinary schools to meet special needs across the continuum. If the aim is to 'make ordinary schools special' — positive discrimination policies for children with special educational needs must be expressed in a somewhat different form.

Comment

The analysis in this chapter leads to a view that providing for children with special needs in ordinary schools is not solely about resources. The view is sometimes expressed by mainstream staff — 'Give us the necessary resources and we will provide for children with special needs'. While resources are of crucial importance — of greater significance will be the less tangible aspects of positive discrimination. This can be readily seen within some mainstream schools where attitudes, ethos and educational aims are particularly conducive to meeting special educational needs — often in the absence of any additional LEA resources. Unless and until all ordinary schools are able to work at the level of individual needs, *Making the Ordinary School Special* will need to involve the operation of a principle of positive discrimination within ordinary schools in the distribution of resources for pupils with special needs. It is important to be clear about what a principle of positive discrimination would mean in practice. It would entail an acceptance and acknowledgement that *some* ('special') children should and will receive *more* than other ('normal') children — whatever the overall level of resources happens to be. The corollary of this would be an acceptance that 'normal' children received *less* than those regarded as 'special'. It is not possible to argue that children with special needs should only be integrated within ordinary schools if the education of 'ordinary' children does not 'suffer'/is not affected/is not disadvantaged in some way. Currently 'ordinary' children *are* affected and might be said to 'suffer' because of the fact that children *within special schools* receive more of the *overall* level of resources available to the education service. Resources (like needs) are relative. What is at issue here is not the need for more resources (essential as these might be) but the ethical decisions which have to be made about the way in which resources are distributed. If more resources are required, they are required for all children — not just for those deemed special. The major question to be resolved concerns *values* and not resources.

The principle of positive discrimination is controversial. It needs to be widely discussed amongst all teachers in ordinary schools. However, in terms of policy development such a principle is likely to need to be initiated, developed and monitored at both central government and LEA level rather than left at the level of schools alone.

Moreover, such a system will need to overcome the 'separatism' which is inherent within our present special education system. The theme of developing policies incorporating the principle of positive discrimination, which in turn can enable ordinary schools to provide for children with special needs alongside their peers, is a major challenge within the field of special education. It is also a recurrent theme as special needs policies at the level of the LEA are considered (see chapters 3 to 5).

This chapter began by asking the question 'Can ordinary schools afford to be special?'. Analysis of the social and political forces and of the values and attitudes which operate within our society indicates that it would be somewhat naive to expect ordinary schools, easily and readily to assume responsibility for providing for all children with special needs. Meeting special educational needs is not necessarily in the interests of schools, given the many factors competing for priority consideration and resources *and* the existence of a separate system for providing for such pupils. It is not surprising then, that schools will sometimes show a reluctance to develop 'integrated' provision for particular groups of children with special needs, even when adequate resourcing is available. Secondary schools will want to avoid developing an image in their community as a school — 'good with the slow learners but not stretching the bright kids'. When such an image prevails there is often anxiety that 'middle class' parents will look elsewhere.

Shapiro (1980) makes the following comments when discussing the social and economic constraints on reform in special education . . .

> While we do not dismiss the importance of educational pressure groups and innovators as catalyst for change, our belief is that the extent of the change depends, in the final analysis, not on the perseverance and commitment of these individuals or groups, but on the parameters set by the social and economic structure. Special education reform, like other areas of educational change, may proceed only to the extent that it is congruent with the needs or goals of that structure.

Yet the social and economic determinism implied here seems to provide an altogether too pessimistic view of the possibilities for radical change. Currently there is a 'revolution in ideas' concerning the nature and purposes of special education. The notion that 20 per cent of the child population are likely to have special educational needs is now a familiar one. If 'specialness' is judged in terms of educational failure and if educational success is synonymous with the possession of examination credentials — why stop at 20 per cent? Warnock's 20 per cent is but a short step from the '40 per cent' of pupils who leave our secondary school system with no negotiable qualifications after twelve years of compulsory schooling. Are 40 per cent of the child population 'special'? As the possibility is revealed that the educational system provides a form of 'guaranteed failure' for other than a small minority of academically able pupils — changes must occur. Tackling the absurdity of a system that fails 40 per cent will inevitably involve tackling the absurdity of regarding 20 per cent of the school population as special, rather than as an extension of individual differences amongst children.

Chapter 3

'Whole Authority' Approaches to Special Educational Needs

'Separation Throughout'

Imagine for one moment that you are a visiting educationalist from overseas. You are interested in examining 'integration' or 'mainstreaming' as it works in Great Britain and you arrive clutching your copy of Warnock and the 1981 Act. You begin your enquiry at the DES where you are directed to speak to a DES official in Schools Branch II. You learn that, as well as special education, Schools Branch II is, curiously, also responsible for architects and buildings, vocational education and 'disadvantage'. Alongside and separate from Schools Branch II is Schools Branch I — responsible for primary and secondary education. This division of responsibility is, you are informed, mirrored, in large part, within Her Majesty's Inspectorate. Each region of the country is served by specialist inspectors for *special education* who work alongside, and in some respects separately from, *phase* and *subject* inspectors. Special education in Great Britain is, apparently, viewed as a phase of education akin to primary or secondary education.

Next stop, the headquarters of a friendly, local education authority office. Here the receptionist guides you through the carefully constructed barriers of an open plan office. You speak to an Assistant Education Officer ('*special* services'). You learn that this individual is totally responsible for all of the administrative aspects of special education in this authority. The AEO (special) is one of three senior administrative officers — the other two dealing with *primary* and *secondary* education. The AEO points to a burgeoning tray of statements waiting to be signed and complains that the legislation has doubled the administrative workload of the job. Time is short here. There are many demands on the administrator's time. Later that day the AEO must attend a *Special Services Sub-committee* meeting to put the case for a further increase in spending on non-teaching assistants to meet the demands of statementing, the Act, etc, etc. You are guided swiftly past the offices of the AEO's *primary and secondary* to the LEA's advisory section. Here you meet the Adviser for *Special* Education. The Adviser seems, if anything, as much under pressure as the AEO. There is, it is explained, a massive in-service job to be done on all teachers within ordinary *primary* and *secondary* schools and the Special Needs Adviser is spearheading the authorities' initiatives in this area. In spite of the cut-backs, the Education Committee has agreed to the appointment of two new special needs advisory posts and a range of new teaching posts to support ordinary schools in meeting special educational needs. The advisory teachers will work with the Adviser for Special Needs and take a major role in the development of INSET training programmes. Together with the other additional teaching posts they will form a new *special needs support service* — accountable to, and orchestrated by, the Adviser and AEO (*Special* Services). The immediate priorities for the Adviser are the drawing up of job descriptions and the scheduling of interview arrangements.

Lunch time in the staff canteen. An unscheduled opportunity to meet up with the advisers for primary and secondary education. Discussion ensues about the proposed new 'special needs advisory service' and the problems of finding teachers who can carry out advisory and supportive work in mainstream schools. You take the opportunity of asking for some suggestions about mainstream primary and secondary schools within the authority who are regarded as examples of 'good practice' in meeting special educational needs. Your question is referred to and answered by the Special Needs Adviser.

Your imaginary visit could have taken you to a variety of other venues. To university departments and institutes of education; to LEA-based teacher centres, and, of course, to mainstream schools themselves. The suggestion here is that all, or most, of the structures and organizations which currently underpin our special educational system are characterized by their separation from mainstream structures. Thus, whether we look at the structure of the DES, the organization of in-service training or the administrative and advisory system of LEAs, special educational needs are characteristically the concern of somebody outside of mainstream primary and secondary education (see table 2).

Not surprisingly, separation of roles and responsibilities is fre-

Table 2: 'Separation Throughout'

		Special Structures	Mainstream Structures
1	DES	Schools Branch II HMI — Special	Schools Branch I HMI — Subject and Phase
2	LEA (a) Committee structure	'Special' Sub-committee	Primary/Secondary/FE Sub-committees
	(b) Finance	Special schools and special education budgets	Budgets for primary/ secondary/etc.
	(c) Administrators	AEO (Special)	AEO (Secondary) AEO (Primary) etc.
	(d) Advisory	Advisers/inspectors for special education	Advisers/inspectors — phase and subject areas
3	Universities/ institutes of higher education	Departments/teams — 'special educational needs'	Departments/teams — phase/curriculum/ discipline areas
4	Schools	Teachers responsible for 'remedial'/special education 'S' salary allowances	Class/subject area teachers

quently found within the organization of schools themselves. Here, in the world of 'special needs departments' and 'special needs coordinators', special education can assume the same identity as a *subject*, rather than being seen as an aspect of *all* subjects and *all* curriculum areas. At the level of schools the problem with this kind of separatist thinking is becoming clearer. There are two current buzz phrases in the field of special educational needs ... — *'whole school approaches'* and *'all teachers are teachers of children with special educational needs'*. Underlying both phrases is the view that meeting special needs should not be seen as the exclusive responsibility of certain designated teachers who hold responsibility posts in this area. The implications of this kind of thinking involve a radical departure from traditional teacher roles and traditional forms of organizing support in mainstream schools. However, this is rarely, if ever, reflected in the organization of services at LEA level or within institutes of higher education, let alone within the DES. Arguably, the organization of special needs provision *within* ordinary schools should be 'mirrored' by the organization of services within the LEA's administrative, advisory and committee structures. If the aim is to have a 'whole school approach' involving devolution of special needs resources and responsibilities to all teachers and to all curriculum areas, then, arguably, this should be reflected at the level of LEA organization. Yet finding a coherent 'whole authority' approach to special educational needs, within LEAs in England and Wales, can only be likened to the legendary quest for the elusive Holy Grail! None of this can be regarded as surprising. Service organization within LEAs has developed within a conceptual framework which links special education to the existence and operation of a separate special schools system. Special schools have been seen to have their own set of needs — staffing, resourcing, curriculum, training and career development. These needs have historically been regarded as having little in common with the needs of the mainstream sector. Headteachers of special schools have wanted someone to represent 'their' views and needs within the LEA. This has contributed to the appointment of officers within the LEA, frequently recruited from the ranks of headteachers of special schools, who have responsibility for special needs. Separation within schools has begot separation within LEAs. This has seemed, until now, to be unproblematic and, indeed, in the natural order of things. Post-Warnock and post-1981 Act, LEAs have, quite naturally, turned to these separate structures when seeking to meet the 'new challenge' of extending the concept of special education into mainstream schools. Thus, 'the special educators' (specialist teachers, psychologists, special education advisers) are expected to move from their knowledge base (derived largely from experience of separate special schools and units, and programme planning for categorized groups of special children in special environments), to the largely alien environment of mainstream education. It is here that the problems begin. We attempt to deal with new concepts and new provisions with old structures and old methods of service organization. For instance a 'transplant' or 'limpet' (Jones, N. 1983) model is used as special education moves into the mainstream. We take what we know — a separate system of meeting special educational needs — and attempt to attach it, limpet like, to the mainstream sector. The people in the LEA organization responsible for this, are, of course, those from the special educational system — 'special' advisers, 'special' administrators and educational psychologists. Sometimes this group is seen to require supplementary support. New posts may emerge — advisers for special educational needs (ordinary schools) or, more often, new advisory special needs support services (Gipps and Goldstein, 1984). Further additions are thus made to the essentially separate special educational structures. The personnel who make up the additions to the structure may demarcate a territorial area and then perceive a need for increasing resources within that area. The adviser special needs (ordinary schools) will eventually require a number of advisory teachers (special needs) to supplement the INSET/school support work which emerges! Thus, in responding to mainstream special needs, the approaches tried and tested within the special educational world are introduced and the dualistic approach — special and mainstream — is reintroduced. Sayer (1985) comments that, 'the history of special schooling looks like the sheds and garages of a cellarless suburban backyard, acquired and added on in bits without ever contemplating a complete rebuild'. The suggestion is that, if ordinary schools are to become special, then the management and organizational structures which underpin special education have to be gradually, progressively and, perhaps painfully, rebuilt. Rebuilding is likely to involve more than the addition of a new 'extension' to the current system. To continue the building analogy, it will involve us in ensuring that the foundations of the mainstream system are strengthened and secured in order to support the development of a new kind of structure.

Developing a 'whole authority' approach to special educational needs is likely to involve a close analysis of the roles and functions of all administrators, all advisers, all HMIs and all teacher trainers. Jones, N. (1983) addresses the central issues in the context of initiatives in Oxfordshire. 'If it made no sense to segregate children with special needs, did it make any further sense to continue with "segregated" administrative, advisory and support services? The continued existence of such services, identified as they are with an administrator, advice and support, set apart from the ordinary services for education in general, and existing as a response to past policies of segregation philosophies and practices, tended only to perpetuate the "institution" of segregation'. The aim in developing a 'whole authority' approach must be to design a management and organisational system which minimises the extent to which special education is treated as marginal to and separate from the management of mainstream education.

Developing a Whole Authority Approach — Barriers to Change

A 'whole authority' approach to special needs would need to involve two major elements.

(i)   *The existence of a policy* on special educational needs, *agreed* by all parties concerned. Such a policy would need to constitute a framework for *action* and active planning as well as a statement of ideals and intentions.

(ii) An active involvement of all advisory/administrative and elected members within an LEA, in the construction, development and realization of policy.

Few (if any) LEAs in England and Wales are likely to have developed 'whole authority' approaches to special educational needs. The reasons are many and various but relate largely to aspects of the way in which special education has been organized in Great Britain. Two critical issues of concern are the ownership of special education and the fragmentation of LEA Services.

'The Ownership' of Special Education

The ownership of special education is a central issue in considering the development of a 'whole authority' approach. Currently, special education is owned by the special educators. It is not owned by mainstream schools and mainstream teachers. The special educators are the array of teaching, advisory, psychological and administrative staff who operate sometimes within, but nevertheless independently of, mainstream schools. It is these individuals who own the *responsibility* for special educational needs and who own and control the *resources* for meeting special needs. While the education Act 1981 has conferred certain responsibilities upon the governing bodies of all ordinary schools, the headteacher of a normal school can still 'refer' a child (and the responsibility for that child) to a separate system which he/she, as a head, *does not own*.

The dualism and segregation which occurs throughout the educational system — at both the level of the DES and the LEA — is intimately linked to the issue of ownership. LEAs are, as we have seen, effectively more responsible for meeting special educational needs than for meeting any other kind of educational need. They have greater ownership of the problem of meeting special needs than ordinary schools themselves, and greater ownership of the special resources. Not surprisingly, when we consider the development of provision for children with special needs within ordinary schools, LEA administrative and advisory officers will want to exert greater control and direction over that provision than they might for other kinds of resource. This contributes to the 'limpet' approach to special education. The control efforts of the LEA are more likely to lead to a special unit approach — a special school in miniature — than to the development of whole school policies. LEAs will want to be able to 'see' the additional resources being provided — to protect them and to ensure that they reach the special children for whom they were intended. The LEA's ownership of special education, combined with the history in Great Britain of separate provision being made predominantly in separate special schools, has produced an LEA financial, administrative and advisory system which is itself often segregated from the mainstream. Within this separate structure, new specialisms and new areas of expertise have blossomed. The isolation of special education from mainstream education has led to the view that teachers in special education have different expertise, employ a different curriculum and have different training and career needs from their mainstream colleagues. This framework of differentiation also lends itself to differentials in salaries for special educational teachers (Burnham 's' allowances) and to a separate management system.

Within the separate management system of special education, vested interests in retaining that separatism inevitably develop. Patricia Potts (1983), has drawn attention to the ways in which the various professionals involved in special education would be effected by a move towards a more integrated system.

> If a policy of integration were implemented, significant features of the present system would disappear or at least be disastrously reduced: initial referral, transfer, formal assessment, the persuasion of unwilling parents to accept segregated education for their children. The professionals that this would affect most are those who are most concerned with assessment and referral — the psychologists, school doctors, head teachers. The planning of services by local authorities would also be transformed affecting the work of inspectorates and advisory staff, who have often made their mark in the past by proliferating segregated provisions ... The jobs done by many professionals thus depend upon the dual system. The more a job involves decisions about moving children between the two parts of the system, or carrying out a plan of action in tailor made seclusion, the more the duality justifies the job, and the less easy it would be to accept integration.

Vested interests are not peculiar to the field of special education. They operate in any system which is under pressure to change. They usually do not represent an intention to deliberately block or prevent change. Rather, as in the case of special education, the attempts of those within the system to retain the status quo are usually based upon their past experiences within special education, which have led to a sincere belief that old practices and provisions were successful. Further, they are based on the belief that the children concerned will be disadvantaged by moves towards a more integrated system. Brennan (1982) talks of 'natural human inertia' as being one factor which prevents radical change in the field of special education.

> ... inertia is not necessarily a wholly bad thing. In many administrators, teachers and parents it is supported by their knowledge of the schools' system. They are aware of the fine achievements of the special schools, notwithstanding their limitations. And they are also well aware of the absence of facilities for children with special educational needs in the ordinary schools. Their concern for children makes them reluctant to move pupils from situations where they have experienced success to untried situations ...

Vested interests are understandable within a historical context in which special education has been owned and controlled by individuals and groups outside of mainstream education. The challenge for the development of a 'whole authority' approach to special needs must, in part at least, involve considering how the ownership of special educational needs and the ownership of the resources for meeting these needs can be passed from the special sector to the mainstream sector.

Fragmentation Within LEAs

Even *within* an LEA's special educational machinery there is frequently conflict of roles and fragmentation of responsibilities. Conflict between advisers for special education and educational psychologists is rarely documented but seems to be both widespread and acute in many LEAs. Educational psychologists are increasingly concerned to move away from an emphasis on working at the level of the individual child — from a direct and 'reactive' service to individual problems and crises — to a systems-oriented role which is more indirect and pro-active. Within the area of special educational needs, in-service education and an *advisory* role vis-à-vis schools and the LEA, often become the twin targets of educational psychologists working within this model. Thus, educational psychologists find themselves squarely within the traditional territory of LEA advisers and inspectors. The problem is not caused simply by some kind of unilateral role redefinition on the part of psychologists. The difficulty begins at the level of the traditional assessment role with individual children. Educational psychologists are, in the main, employed by LEAs to identify and assess the needs of individual 'handicapped' children. In assessing and spelling out for an LEA the nature of an individual child's needs, and in offering advice to the LEA on what is required to meet those needs, educational psychologists must have a fundamental concern for LEA *provision* for *all* children with special needs. If we then ask the question, *'Who should advise* an LEA on its provision for meeting special educational needs?', we again open up the possibility of serious rifts between educational psychologists on the one hand, and advisers/inspectors for special educational needs on the other. Sometimes, the potential for conflict is minimized by the particular personal qualities and interactions of the individual postholders concerned. Nevertheless, it is unlikely that anyone would set out to design a management system with such an in-built potential for conflict concerning roles.

Fragmentation and conflict within an LEA is not limited to educational psychologists and advisers. Schools will also be familiar with splits between 'remedial' and 'special' advisory staff — often working to different echelons of the LEA hierarchy. Some LEAs have multiplied this fragmentation by creating an array of support staff, linked to supposedly discreet groups of children with special needs (for example, specific learning difficulties, 'statemented pupils' etc.), each working from different bases and each responsible to different advisory and administrative officers within an authority.

The absence of a coordinated approach within an LEA usually acts to limit the development of coherent LEA policies which, in turn, enable active planning to occur. Fragmentation affects the sense of direction and the job satisfaction of the various services involved and has important implications for ordinary (and special) schools. Headteachers and staff of ordinary schools first have to learn to deal with a system which is separate from the resource and support system of mainstream education. Then, the second task involves picking their way through the separate structures of that system to find the particular service which seems to relate or respond to their needs. The irony is that, at the end of this exercise, characterized as it is by areas of specialism and specialization, there is likely to be an expectation that the ordinary class teacher will need to respond to whatever needs are identified.

Towards a Whole Authority Approach to Special Educational Needs

The view developed in this chapter is that the aim of making ordinary schools special is only likely to be fully realized where there exists a whole authority framework which encourages and facilitates this aim. It is argued here, that the organization of LEA special needs services should 'mirror' the desired organization of special needs provision within ordinary schools. Traditional forms of remedial or special provision, in which the remedial/special teacher took responsibility for 'her/his' pupils and taught them in a system separate from mainstream teachers, have provided the model for a parallel pattern of LEA organization. Special administrative and special educational advisory staff take responsibility for 'their' teachers, 'their' schools and 'their' resources. Increasingly, the idea of whole school approaches and the collective responsibility of all teachers for meeting special educational needs is being expressed within ordinary schools. New roles are being proposed for special needs staff. The idea of special needs teachers operating as 'coordinators' and as 'support staff' — facilitating the involvement and responsibilities of all teachers in meeting special needs — is gaining ground. In essence, developments at the school level entail a movement away from specialization of teacher roles and towards more generic patterns of responsibility, management, organization and mutual support. The idea that teachers in the area of special educational needs possess an exclusive form of expertise gives way to a model which assumes that all teachers can make an appropriate response to children with difficulties, given appropriate resources and support. The emphasis is placed upon the similarities shared by special children and special teachers with their non-special peers rather than upon their differences. We can recognize that the development of a 'whole school' approach to meeting special needs is hindered by those patterns of school organization and perceptions of teacher roles which work to place responsibility for special needs, exclusively on the shoulders of certain members of staff, i.e. remedial/special needs teachers. In the same way, the organization of LEA services and the roles performed by 'special' personnel, can work against the involvement of all administrators and advisory staff. Few, if any, LEAs have developed a system whereby subject and phase (primary/secondary) advisers or inspectors have real involvement in the area of special educational needs. Visits by such staff to special schools and units are often rare, even within an LEA where their involvement is actively encouraged by colleagues within the special education field. Similarly, subject and phase advisers rarely make significant contributions to training and in-service programmes for teachers with special needs responsibilities. Just as the expertise and curriculum of mainstream education is lost to children within segregated special provision, so is the active involvement of the LEA's advisory network. 'Mainstream' advisers will rarely be involved in the appointment of teaching staff to special schools, special units or, indeed, with mainstream special needs' facilities. Probationary teachers, entering the special needs field, are often supervised by special rather than subject/phase advisers. Should not the aim be to make 'all advisers advisers of children with special needs?'

As we have seen, the roles of LEA administrators can show a similar pattern of segregated responsibilities. The sine qua non of administrators must be to evolve an efficient and cost effective system of organization. From such a perspective it must be tempting to view special education as a neat and tidy area of administrative responsibility. The complexities and paperwork of the 1981 Act further encourages the separation of administrative duties. Thus, a pattern typically emerges in many authorities of AEO (Secondary); AEO (Primary) and AEO (Special). While such divisions of responsibility may seem to make administrative sense, within a largely segregated special educational system, they are unlikely to be conducive to the development of non-segregation policies. Take for instance, the problem of administrators developing sensitivity to the resourcing issues involved in meeting special needs in ordinary schools. *What ordinary schools require is a continuity of administrative response to their resourcing needs.* It is patently unhelpful to schools when needs, which lie on a continuum, have to be referred to a different administrative officer who is not part of, or party to, the resourcing of all pupils and all needs in the school. 'All administrators are administrators for special educational needs'.

No single pattern of service organization could meet the requirements of all LEAs. However, what is being suggested here is that 'whole authority' approaches to special needs would be characterized by the progressive development of structures, and forms of organization, in which the roles of all administrators and all advisers are broadened to include clear responsibilities towards children with special educational needs. This would, necessarily, entail a transfer of *exclusive* special needs responsibilities, from special educational advisory and administrative staff to their mainstream colleagues. Thus there would be an involvement from all administrators, for example, in the 1981 Act statementing procedures and the resourcing of special needs provisions. In the process authorities could 'absorb' any separate special, administrative officers and, thereby, increase the personnel concerned with the secondary and primary phases. Each administrator would then carry a dual responsibility (for example, secondary/special; primary/special) albeit for a reduced number of schools. Similarly, there would be an involvement of all advisers in the selection of staff, the induction, training and career development of special needs teaching staff. The corollary of such transfers of responsibility would, of course, be a broadening of the roles of existing special administrators and advisers and an equal involvement in 'non-special' areas of administrative and advisory work. This would, to some extent, mirror the developments occurring within special needs provisions in ordinary schools. Here, 'coordinators' are expected to work across the curriculum, across subject boundaries, and themselves, to make a contribution to mainstream teaching. The suggestion is not that LEAs have no need of the input of individuals with a background of training, experience and interest within the field of special needs. Rather, that the deployment of their skills and expertise should be seen as a resource, to enrich and enhance the involvement of all those involved in meeting children's special needs. An incidental, but important, consequence of such a move, would be the extension and widening of career opportunities for the 'special educators' themselves. Within our current system the Adviser for Special Education has as much opportunity of becoming the Chief Adviser for an LEA as the AEO (Special) has of becoming the Chief Education Officer and as the Head of Remedial, in a school, has of becoming a headteacher!

The development of integrated administrative and advisory structures, at the level of the LEA, which reflect a desired pattern of provision, at the level of schools, might in turn be seen to have consequences for the organization of structures within the DES, within HMI and within the field of teacher training at institutes of higher education. How, for instance, might the respective roles of HMIs within the phase/subject and special boundaries be worked out, within a more integrated structure? What might be the implications, for teacher training, of integrating the special needs structures within universities and colleges of higher education, with curriculum-based structures?

The steps being proposed, involving as they do significant changes in the job and role requirements of individuals, are only likely to evolve over an extended period of time. LEAs wishing to develop a more integrated provision for children with special needs may, in the short term, be hindered by the existence of a large, segregated, special school system. In a similar way, movements towards a 'whole authority' organization may be hindered by the nature and existence of current administrative and advisory posts. However, opportunities for change and redevelopment continually occur within an LEA organization and the long term aim, of developing a 'whole authority' approach, could be incrementally achieved.

At present, the main priority for LEAs might be to *coordinate* their existing separate advisory systems. This might, at least, enable some kind of coherence to emerge in the field of special education policy. The development of a special needs policy within an LEA, which would provide some sense of direction to both ordinary and special schools, is frequently hindered by the absence of a coordinated approach to planning and policy making within the LEA. Coordination of services, particularly the coordination of special educational advisory and school psychological services, is a controversial area.

A small number of LEAs in Great Britain have, historically, achieved some measure of coordination in this area by making educational psychologists responsible, also, for the authority's special education advisory service. An even smaller number have attempted to achieve coordination by bringing the school psychology service under the auspices of a special educational adviser or inspector. The majority of LEAs exist with an organization in which there are often tensions, conflict and unease between these two groups. Coordination, by which is meant the bringing together of separate psychological and special educational advisory services into a unified system, is likely to involve a perceived loss of autonomy by educational psychologists, advisers or both. However, such coordination is long overdue in many LEAs. The field of special educational needs is analagous to the tentacles of an octopus. Developing a coherent policy, a sense of direction and movement, requires a measure of influence and control over each of the tentacles. If one tentacle — for example the policy and practices of an SPS — is moving in one direction, while others — policy on statements, provision and resources and INSET — are moving in another, the results are predictable. The octopus makes little perceptible movement in any direction at all.

While coordination may facilitate the development of LEA policies, it must be regarded as only an intermediate step towards a whole authority system. The latter would involve the further integration of the coordinated, special structures into mainstream systems.

Comment

The final goal of a 'whole authority' approach to special educational needs must be a situation in which both the responsibility and the resources for meeting special needs are devolved to, and owned by, ordinary schools themselves. Such a goal may never be fully realized. Arguably, however, the principle of increasing mainstream schools' ownership of special education should guide LEAs, each and every time a decision has to be made concerning the allocation and management of special resources. Decisions about the accountabilities and responsibilities of special staff should reflect this principle, in answering questions such as — Is the member of staff responsible to individuals within special education or mainstream education? Is the person responsible to the headteacher of an ordinary school, or to some central structure within the LEA?

There are some indications within a number of LEA's in Great Britain, of movements in this direction. Initiatives such as the Banbury Project in Oxfordshire (Jones, N. 1983; Sayer 1983 and 1985) have begun to uncover both the potential, and the inherent difficulties, of such an approach. The Banbury Project involves the grouping of schools to form 'sectors' (one or more secondary schools and accompanying feeder primaries) to which special resources can be allocated and shared. Decisions are made by sector-based staff — headteachers, administrators and support service personnel — about the use and distribution of resources. The 'sector' model represents a powerful and important step in this field. However, the idea of 'sectors' as forming the focus for the delivery of special educational resources and services, is unlikely to gain much momentum if it is restricted to meeting special needs alone. Sectors will need to have planning and management realities beyond the field of special needs. At its most radical, the approach would involve headteachers and senior teaching staff, of all schools, taking responsibility *across schools* and *stages* of education, for the development of all pupils in the community served by a sector. The sector approach approximates closely to the idea in the ILEA's Fish Report (1985) of 'clustering' together groups of ordinary schools, within a geographical area along with specialist provisions, peripatetic and support services. The idea of 'clusters', fits within the Report's suggestion that, 'the principle aim of changes should be to delegate responsibilities within firm guidelines established by the authority to the nearest practical point of service delivery'. The Fish Report stops short of delegation of decision making to headteachers of ordinary schools — leaving instead decisions about assessment, placement and resourcing to a 'divisional management group' (administrators, inspectors, psychologists etc). Ultimately, a situation could be envisaged in which the management of special facilities of all kinds — including off-site units and special schools — became a part of the management of ordinary schools. Movements of this kind do not entail any abrogation of responsibility on the part of the LEA for the formulation of *policy*. Localized management by mainstream schools can only make sense within a framework of LEA guidelines concerning policy and provision for children with special needs. Such guidelines would spell out agreed aims, broad directions and, perhaps, minimum standards, within which schools developed their provision and deployed their resources.

The steps proposed in this chapter, involving, as they do, the movement of the ownership of special education towards mainstream education, are fraught with possible dangers. Are mainstream schools ready to accept full responsibility for children with special educational needs? Are the teachers and heads of ordinary schools in a position to protect the interests of a vulnerable group of children and to maintain an adequate level of resourcing to meet their needs? Questions such as these cannot be satisfactorily answered by changes in resource policies, alterations in the organization of LEA services or, indeed, by passing the management responsibility for special resources to mainstream schools. Ultimately, such changes might assist ordinary schools in responding to a wider range of special educational needs. However, the realization of this ideal is crucially dependent upon a shared framework, and a shared policy at all levels of the education service based upon an acceptance of diversity and an equal valuing of children with special needs. Within such a framework the protection of resources for children with special needs would no longer be an issue.

Chapter 4

To 'Statement' or Not to 'Statement' — That is the Question?

Opinions vary enormously about the use and usefulness of 'statements' of special educational needs. For some, they are seen as providing a solution to the problem of obtaining resources for children with special needs. For this group, the only shortcoming of statementing is seen to be the time taken by LEAs to compile and issue them. For others, statements are regarded as, at best, a necessary cross to bear, and at worst, a hindrance in the field of special educational needs. Given this diversity of opinion, it is not surprising that local education authorities vary in the extent to which formal, section 5 assessments and statements are used. Some authorities are regarded, and known, as pursuing 'low-statementing policies' (for example, Oxfordshire — see Hackney, 1985). In others, rigid adherence to the formal legislative procedures is seen as being the only approach to developing provision for children with special educational needs. Similar differences probably occur within mainstream schools. Some headteachers will have used statements as the route to extra resources and, certainly, as an important method of registering the schools 'special needs' with the LEA. Others may view the lengthy bureaucratic procedures as being prohibitive, and the likely outcomes as being segregational.

The particular direction taken by LEAs with regard to statementing is crucial for any policy aimed at 'making ordinary schools special'. It will be argued in this chapter that the justification for the use of statements is unclear, and that their wholesale and injudicious use may, in the long term, prove to be both divisive and unhelpful to schools, to parents and to children with special needs.

Statements — Warnock and the 1981 Act

The idea of multidisciplinary assessments of special needs (under section 5 the 1981 Act) leading to the production of statements (under section 7), originated in the deliberations of the Warnock Report. Warnock first presented the concept of special educational needs as lying along a continuum. Then, immediately, the Committee shattered its conceptual clarity by introducing the notion of recording 'some children' along this continuum and not others. Warnock's decision, that some children needed to be recorded as in need of special educational provision, was arrived at after some considerable soul searching.

> We have considered most carefully whether such a system of recording could in practice tend to emphasize the separateness of the children concerned — an idea which throughout this report we are at pains to dispel ... However, to the extent that a system of recording may suggest a form of separateness we think that any possible disadvantages are outweighed by two considerations of practical importance. In the first place the needs of children who require the provision of regular special help outside the ordinary school greatly exceed those children for whom special provision can be made wholly or mainly within the school — they call for greater resources and a more complex organization of services. Unless these needs and the corresponding means of meeting them are explicitly recorded there will be a real danger of insufficiency or default in their provision. Secondly, even though regular specialist help may be available to the ordinary school which a child is attending there can be no guarantee, in the absence of a formulation of need and provision, that it will continue to be available if he moves to another school, whether in the same area or that of another local Authority. (DES, 1978)

The reasoning here seems to be that the formal recording of children with severe and complex disabilities is required for three main reasons. Firstly, because their needs are different in some ways from others who have the kind of special needs which ordinary schools can meet. Secondly, *LEAs cannot be trusted* to provide the necessary resources without some legislative prompts. Thirdly, because of the problems of guaranteeing continuity of special provision. The first reason is curiously at odds with the idea of a continuum of special needs and, with Warnock's clear intent to, 'eliminate the

notion of two types of children — the handicapped and the nc
handicapped'. The remaining reasons are intimately linked to tl
recurring idea of the need for protection of children with special
needs. The need to protect and safeguard the interests of children with
severe, complex or long-term disabilities was then embodied within
the 1981 Act and accompanying circular. 'The Act lays down formal
procedures for the assessment of children whose needs are, or probably are, such as to require LEAs to determine their special educational provision, as it gives children with such needs the protection of a
statement' (DES, Circular 1/83).

The 1981 Act criteria for who should be statemented are closely
linked (if not synonymous) with the provision of *extra* resources.
According to the circular which accompanied the Act there are three
groups of children to whom the 'Secretary of State expects LEAs to
afford the protection of a statement'.

1 Those children attending special schools.
2 Those children placed in special units attached to an ordinary
   school.
3 Those children who have severe or complex learning difficulties which require the provision of *extra resources* in ordinary
   schools.

Thus, Circular 1/83 suggests that formal procedures should be initiated, 'where there are prima facie grounds to suggest that a child's
needs are such as to require provision additional to, or otherwise
different from, the facilities and resources generally available in ordinary schools in the area under normal arrangements'. This, of course,
immediately poses two questions. What level of provision is 'normally available in ordinary schools' and what counts as 'extra'? Thus, an
LEA which has a favourable level of basic resourcing and/or utilizes a
positive discrimination system of resourcing for children with special
needs (see Chapter 5) could have considerably less need to statement
pupils than another authority. In addition, the Act allows seemingly
unlimited discretion in what is considered 'extra'. Inexplicably children who attend disruptive units or reading centres are not regarded as
receiving anything extra! Circular 1/83 also draws a distinction between special provision made by ordinary schools, 'from their own
resources' (where no formal procedures are required) and special provision 'determined by the LEAs' (where they are). Resources are,
therefore, seen to be 'owned' either by the school or by the LEA, and
the application of different statutory rules is dependent upon that
ownership. This presumably opens the way for two opposing paths

for any authority. One would be to reduce the number of statemented children by handing over the 'ownership' of special resources to schools themselves. The second, would be to increase the number of statemented pupils by declaring an increasing range of resources to be 'extra' in some way, for example, peripatetic support, specialist equipment, etc. To some extent the minimal and maximal approaches to statementing being pursued by LEAs in England and Wales are following one or other of these two paths.

The Case Against Statementing

Whatever the intentions of both the Warnock Committee and the DES, a number of perhaps unintended consequences have followed from the imposition of a 'recording' or 'statementing' division upon the continuum of special educational needs.

The Focus on Procedures

Some months after the introduction of the 1981 Act legislation, a member of HMI in the field of special needs was heard to comment that it was becoming impossible to get a sensible word out of educational psychologists about special education because they had become, 'obsessed with the minutiae of the formal procedures of assessment and statementing'. Certainly, the practical necessity for LEAs to implement the procedures of the Act led to a great deal of frenzied activity that was not restricted solely to educational psychologists. Information documents, new forms for 'advice' giving and letters to parents appeared, almost overnight, and were scattered like confetti within, and between, LEAs. Complex, procedural flow-charts were published in educational journals (for example, Waterman, 1983). In some cases 'the procedures' seemed to achieve a reality and justification of their own. At times, it appeared as though the reason why the child needed a statement in the first place had been largely forgotten. This emphasis on procedures switched the spotlight of the 1981 Act onto the issue of assessing the '2 per cent', as opposed to *providing* for Warnock's continuum of needs.

Resourcing the Procedures

If a statement is to be drawn-up on a pupil, by an LEA, then the child must first be assessed under section 5 arrangements. If a statement is maintained then it must be annually reviewed and a reassessment carried out by the LEA in the year after the child reaches the age of 13½. The professional, administrative and clerical work required to implement these procedures is considerable. Thus, the Act's requirement that educational psychologists participate in the assessment and reassessment procedures has led to a cry from many principal educational psychologists for increases in the staffing of their services. New administrative and advisory posts have appeared in many LEAs as a direct result of the need to 'resource the procedures'. This process reaches its pinnacle in an LEA with the appointment of a 'Statementing Officer'. Thus, in an educational climate of contracting resources, the few resources available to an LEA may come to be spent upon manning the bureaucracy of statement production.

The Focus on Assessment

Access to the protection of a statement comes via assessment, and what is referred to in many LEAs as an MDA (Multidisciplinary Assessment). MDAs occur when an LEA feels that there exists prima facie grounds for a formal assessment under section 5 of the Act — rather than when a child might be considered to require medical or psychological input. The two are not always synonymous. Why should we view, for instance, children who are slow to learn and require considerable small group help and particular kinds of educational input, as in need of medical or psychological investigation? For years the use of the old medical report forms (SE2) has been something of an embarrassment to clinical medical officers when used for the majority of children with special needs. Completed SE2 forms and the newly devised 'medical advice' forms contain little of note for most children who are slow in acquiring basic skills or who pose a range of social behavioural difficulties in schools. Similarly, the 'advice' provided by educational psychologists is usually singularly lacking in useful information which is distinctive and different from that provided by teachers. This is not a criticism of the doctors and educational psychologists as advice givers, but of the mistaken notion that educational failure, of itself, requires medical and psychological investigation. Again, the procedures that might be appropriate for a handicapped minority of children with special needs are applied inappropriately without regard to need, to other children.

Those committed to the use of MDAs and formal statements may argue that only by careful assessments of needs will individual pupils receive the 'correct' form of special provision. Such a view ignores the realities of LEA decision-making procedures. It will be an exceptional administrator who examines the minute details provided by the professional advice givers before placement decisions are made. Meeting individual needs is more likely to be governed by the 'primacy of provision' principle. In the absence of powerful and insistent parental pressure, the pattern of existing provision in an LEA dictates, perhaps understandably, the outcomes of MDAs. It will prove impossible, in the main, for administrators, advisers and psychologists to be unaffected by these constraints. Usually, neither the financial resources nor the necessary elements of provision will exist, which will be sufficiently flexible to meet individual needs. Thus, LEAs will continue to identify and assess children who require provision which does not exist in the form, or the place, where it is required. The focus upon assessment is unlikely to reverse the well-known tendency for LEAs to fit children to available provision. In its most extreme form this tendency can lead to the placement of individual pupils being determined by the availability of existing transport to a special school, rather than any consideration of assessed needs! The problem with statements is that, by focussing on assessment procedures, we pay lip service to the identification of individual needs while the system remains largely unchanged, and dominated by existing provision. 'Assessment' can effectively become a mechanism for avoiding issues of provision. The alternative would be to develop provision to avoid the need for individual assessments of need (see chapter 5). Procedures such as MDA represent the ultimate step in a whole sequence of assessment of special needs. Warnock's oft quoted 'five stages of assessment' begin with classroom-based identification procedures by ordinary teachers, and proceed through to the full-blown extravaganza of MDA. Thus, the focus on assessment in the statementing procedures is linked to an emphasis on identification and assessment at the school level. Identification and assessment procedures in schools themselves produce a number of unintended consequences. Tutt (1985) comments, 'this widespread process of identification, whilst intended to be helpful, in practice leads to increased pressure for rejection rather than integration'. Schools are led into the situation of 'finding' (identifying) and then assessing, 'their 20 per cent'. Again the emphasis is placed upon the assessment of *children* which is divorced from issues of provision, curricula and teaching methods. It is the 20 per cent of children who are seen to *possess* the special needs. Thus, while categories of disability may have gone as a result of the legislation, the knock-on effect of an emphasis on identification and assessment is, as far as concepts and definitions of special needs are concerned, to retain the status quo.

Conflicts of Interest

In contributing to an MDA, the professional 'advice-givers' (principally teachers, psychologists and doctors) are guided by the legislation to give their advice based upon perceived needs, rather than on available provision. Thus, the use of statements sets the scene for a variety of possible conflicts between the individuals constructing the advice and the administrative officers having to make placement decisions. Such conflicts are not new and cannot be laid solely at the door of the new legislation. The 1981 Act has, however, resurrected important issues amongst groups such as educational psychologists. These issues include the questions, 'Who is the client?' and 'To what extent can educational psychologists operate as advocates for children and parents, while continuing to draw their monthly pay cheque from the local authority?'. Peter Newell (1985) of the Children's Legal Centre, accuses certain LEAs of 'gagging professionals', by constraining them in what they are allowed to say to parents and in their written advice to the LEA '... What those authorities are pretending is that their attempt to gag their professionals is based on the very proper desire to see that advice is not limited by what provision exists in an area, but it's quite obvious by what is happening that the real motivation has nothing whatsoever to do with that. It is because they do not wish to be committed to advice which will become public to the parents, to courses of action which are going to cost money.' Newell exhorts educational psychologists as a group to break loose from the shackles of their employing authority, to insist that their first duty is to their child clients with special needs '... By setting out those needs in an unambiguous, and unfettered, uncontrolled way.' It is likely that the situation is not quite as clear cut as Newell suggests. Similarly, given the lack of consensus about what constitutes a special need, it is questionable whether individual professionals should, or could, comment upon needs outside of some kind of framework of existing provision. Perhaps it is more important to consider ways of providing for individual pupils' special needs which do not entail continual recourse to producing statements. Statementing procedures operate as a kind of appeals procedure for establishing the rights of individual children with special needs, and conflicts of interests appear to be an inherent part of such procedures.

Statements and Their Abuse

At their worst statements can be used by schools, parents and the LEA in ways which can only be regarded as representing an abuse of the system. LEAs can intentionally utilize statements as a method of restricting access to limited resources. Here, statements become the only method whereby schools can register their special needs. In addition, statements force a situation in which such needs have to be related to individual pupils. Then the lengthy procedures involved act effectively as a funnel — slowing down the process by which the LEA responds to those needs. In other situations, 'calling for a statement' can become a tactic, regularly employed by schools, to effectively off-load responsibility for children who are 'difficult to teach'. This can occur particularly where schools are confronted by hostility or criticism from an individual child's parents. Abuse of the statementing procedures can also occur, via the disproportionate influence of certain parental groups within the area of special needs. For instance, one administrative officer was heard to remark flippantly that his priorities in special needs were, 'dyslexics, Downs Syndrome children and the gifted!'. This remark belies a fundamental truth of most legislation in the field of human welfare — namely, that certain groups are better able to extract resources and benefit from legislation, than are others. It is interesting in this respect to note that the first appeal to the courts under the 1981 Act which has overruled an LEA decision, concerns a 'dyslexic' pupil. The suggestion is not that such groups should have no recourse to the legislation, but that the statementing procedures are likely to disproportionately favour articulate, well-informed and resourceful parents who will, understandably, 'use the system' to achieve desired ends for their children. This has to be set in the context of the fact that the majority group of special needs children — those with moderate learning difficulties and social behavioural problems — come almost exclusively from family backgrounds least equipped to 'use the system'.

The Justification for Statements

Statements are generally viewed by schools and LEA officers as a necessary, if not essential, means of *securing* and *protecting* additional resources for children with special needs. In terms of securing resources, LEA administrators will often see themselves as needing to be in the position of having a 'hatful of statements' in order to 'go to committee', to argue for the necessary additional resources. The way in which schools provide 'evidence' of their special needs by referring individual children is mirrored at LEA level. Thus, administrators perceive the need to provide their elected members with 'evidence', in the form of 'number of completed statements'. In at least one LEA in Great Britain all completed statements have to be presented to a sub-committee of elected members (see Conway and Hepworth, 1985). The problems which confront LEA officers in this respect are considerable, and are usually closely related both to the absence of an alternative resource policy, and to the particular concepts of special needs that may prevail in an Authority.

The protection issue is even more complex. The view of LEAs that statements 'protect the interests of children with special needs' is expounded by both central government and HMI. The following questions are, however, rarely if ever addressed. Who is doing the protecting? From what and from whom are they protecting the children? Proponents of the protection viewpoint seem to come close to arguing that some members of the LEA (advisers, psychologists, administrators and teachers within the special needs area) have to protect children with special needs from other members of the LEA (other administrators, advisers, teachers and elected members, etc.). This paradoxical situation does seem to be close to what is actually happening in LEAs at the present time. Statements are used as the legal muscle to secure positive discrimination for children with special needs in the allocation of resources within an authority. If used in this way, LEAs seem to be exercising a peculiar kind of masochism. They employ a costly army of special needs support staff to inflict upon themselves the additional expenditure incurred by the production of an ever increasing number of statements of need. Here, conflict of interest seems to be built into the system. That the interests of handicapped pupils should be protected and safeguarded is not in dispute. What is being suggested is that positive discrimination should not be inflicted on an authority by parts of that authority, but should instead become an explicit part of the policy of the whole authority, and recognized in its resource allocation procedures. Both the 'securing' and 'protection' rationales rest upon a kind of unspoken *mistrust*. Parents of handicapped children may not trust the LEA to ensure that their children's needs are met. Schools may not trust the LEA to adequately resource special needs. LEAs may not trust schools to use resources, allocated to particular individual children, to meet their needs. Mistrust may arise between special administrators, support service staff and their 'non-special' counterparts or, indeed, between elected members and LEA administrative officers. If assessment and statementing procedures have a justification not based solely upon mistrust, then it lies within the area of their potential for settling disagreements between the different parties concerned with meeting an individual child's needs. To some extent the 1981 Act procedures are used in this way. For example, parents and teaching staff may differ in their views about a child's needs. They may disagree as to whether particular services and resources are required. Similar disagreements can and do, occur between schools, support service staff, and LEA administrators. In such situations, some kind of arbitration and decision-making machinery is required. Hopefully the number of such cases would be small within a policy framework where adequate provision is made in cases where there is *agreement* about the nature of a child's needs and the provision required. In this context we would have the necessary safeguards and protection for children with severe and complex needs. Where there was an absence of agreement between any parties concerning the adequacy of provision being made for a child, their parents (or teachers and support personnel working on their behalf) would have access to an arbitration system.

Comment

Statements of special need are enshrined in educationl law. They may well be here to stay, although as we have seen LEAs are allowed an enormous range of discretion concerning when, where and with whom they are used. For many LEA policy-makers, statements represent the major method of obtaining and protecting resources for children with special needs. Many parents view the acquisition of a statement as a guarantee of 'integrated' provision for their child. However, it has been argued in this chapter that the justification for the use of statements is unclear, and seems largely to be based upon a kind of intrinsic mutual mistrust between the various partners concerned, viz, parents schools and LEAs. Consequently, statements are subject to abuse. Even where an LEA draws up statements on pupils within mainstream schools, their effect can be divisive, and work against the principles of integration. The following comment, taken from an article written by an LEA Special Needs Adviser and administrator, is illuminating in this respect.

> It is equally clear that the formal assessment procedures are lengthy — in our case some 6 to 9 months on average — and may not necessarily result in a more appropriate education for some children, nor their acceptance by peers and adults in schools. We are conscious that integration does not automatically result from merely placing children with special needs in a mainstream school — indeed, the extention of the protection of a statement to those in mainstream schools is potentially divisive. (Conway and Hepworth, 1985)

This chapter began with the question — 'To statement or not to statement?'. Clearly, the question cannot be answered in isolation from a series of other questions. For example, 'What is the overall policy in a particular LEA for meeting special educational needs? What resources are considered "normally available" for children with special needs? What positive discrimination policies does the LEA have in the allocation and use of resources for children with special needs? How near are schools to the ideal of providing access to the curriculum for the widest possible range of needs?'. The view expressed here is not that a statement should never be used, but that developing answers to these questions is a far higher priority than the expansion of procedures which will bring an increasing number of pupils into the 'statementing net'.

In reality, of course, many, if not most, LEAs will be a long way from providing answers to such large and fundamental questions. Some may place special educational needs a long way down on their agenda for priority action. For a small minority, special needs may not even feature on any important policy agenda. In these authorities it may appear that the only way forward is via a 'mass-statementing' approach. In the words of one educational psychologist, 'an approach which puts the plight of individual pupils on the politicians laps'. There are two major problems with this approach. Firstly, it is rarely done effectively. Individual pupils scattered across a number of schools are individually presented as requiring statements. Rarely does this get any significant message across to LEAs or to elected members. Consider instead the likely outcome if a number of schools presented a small group of pupils *concurrently* as in need of statements of need. In *all* cases schools would need to make explicit to both parents, and to the LEA, their desire to retain the pupils within the ordinary school — given additional resources. Equally important would be a unanimous and insistent voice from the parents concerned for *both* mainstream provision and additional resources. If this situation were duplicated across a number of schools concurrently the consequences for an authority, adhering rigidly to 1981 Act procedures, would make most LEA administrators tremble! Approaches such as this would be much more effective in demonstrating the nonsense of using statementing as the only mechanism for gaining resources for children with special needs. Other, less drastic, approaches are also available for LEAs to employ in developing provision for special needs. It is, for instance, possible, as an interim step, to deploy resources within ordinary schools for children who might be 'regarded', 'deemed' or 'recorded' as in some way special rather than using statementing procedures. This may provide a politically and administratively more acceptable solution, as part of an evolving policy aimed ultimately at resourcing and predicting needs rather than crisis intervention via the statementing procedures.

The second major objection to mass-statementing approaches is, if anything, of greater significance. Such approaches actively retain and maintain the status quo, in terms of the concepts of special needs which still prevail in, and outside of, schools and education departments. A policy based upon recourse to the production of statements, as a solution to the problems of meeting special educational needs, teaches everyone in the system a particular set of lessons. These are that special needs reside purely within individual children who require assessment and processing; that special needs are someone else's responsibility (the LEA's / the psychologist's / special educator's etc.), and that meeting special educational needs is purely a matter of obtaining the necessary resources. *The greatest danger of statements is their ability to provide powerful and immediate reinforcement to everyone concerned.* Certainly, the production of statements can be seen to meet the short term ends and needs of all partners in the enterprise, including the individual child. Needless to say this immediate reinforcement usually has a long-term cost. In this case the injudicious use of statements confirms outmoded concepts of special educational needs. It thereby acts as a major barrier to the long-term aim of making adequate provision for all children with difficulties.

Chapter 5

Children with Special Needs — Towards a Resourcing Policy

'The integration of children with special needs is all about money and resources'. This is a view likely to be held by many within both mainstream and special education. The notion that money and resources are important in special education seems to contrast sharply with a view of special education as being a matter of humanitarian, caring concern for the handicapped. Yet any analysis of the social, political and ethical context of special education (see chapter 2) indicates clearly the importance of economic factors. Administrators, advisers and psychologists are usually aware of this in their struggles to achieve, at policy level, as large a slice as possible of the educational 'resource cake'. A pervasive and intriguing aspect of special needs policies is the extent to which issues and practices at LEA level are 'mirrored' within schools. Thus, staff with special needs responsibilities in primary and secondary schools are likely to feel an equivalent need to establish special needs as a high priority claim on staffing and material resources within their own schools.

Resource policies are underpinned and guided by more fundamental ethical and value-based decisions concerning how *much* should be spent on *which* pupils in our schools. However, the way in which LEAs deploy, administer and monitor resources is likely to have important implications for the development of non-segregation policies. The development of a resourcing policy is possibly the single most important step which can be taken by any LEA to facilitate the attempts of ordinary schools to accept responsibility for the widest possible range of children. This chapter will focus upon current systems of resourcing special educational needs. The problems which any resourcing system must take into account will be considered. Finally, some possible directions for an alternative policy designed to meet a continuum of special needs will be outlined.

Resourcing Special Needs — Current LEA Policies

Uniform policies within LEAs in Great Britain tend to be the exception rather than the rule. This is as true of resourcing policies for children with special needs as it is of any aspect of the educational system. Wide variations between authorities in the way in which financial resources (teaching and non-teaching staff, money and materials) are organized and allocated can be anticipated. LEA practices in this area are rarely made explicit. They are not externally monitored by the DES, and are only infrequently mentioned in published research. However, while authorities will differ in matters of detail, the 1981 Act Legislation and its associated procedures, as well as DES circulars relating to staffing recommendations, provide the guidelines used by most LEAs for resourcing children with special needs.

Figure 2 illustrates the way in which resourcing policies typically operate. A resource-based division is imposed upon the continuum of special needs. Those children who, for whatever reason, are regarded by an LEA as requiring a statement under the terms of the 1981 Act, usually achieve a considerably higher level of resourcing than children not so regarded. Nationally the proportion of the school population

Figure 2: THE RESOURCE DIVIDE

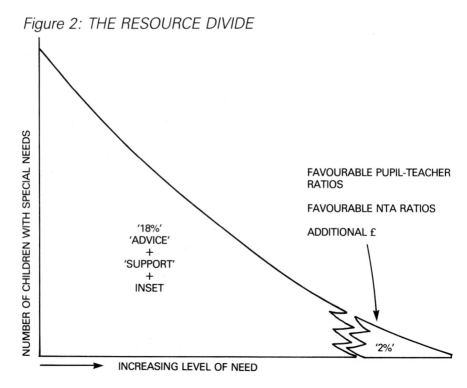

seen as requiring 'resources additional to those normally available in ordinary schools' (DES, 1983) (and thereby, in the eyes of most LEAs, a statement) has averaged around 2 per cent. The majority of the '2 per cent' are likely to attend special schools. The remainder will be located within ordinary schools and receive special provision either individually or, more often, as part of a special unit or class.

Special education is an expensive commodity. This is apparent when we compare the level of resources attributed to 'statemented' and 'non-statemented' pupils. (The latter includes, of course, the so-called '18 per cent' with special needs). Table 3 illustrates this aspect in comparing estimates of unit costs per pupil across primary, secondary and special schools (DES, 1985b).

Another comparison of relative costs can be made by looking at the proportion of the teaching force in an authority engaged in meeting special educational needs in relation to the numbers of children served. The Fish Committee carried out a comprehensive review of provision within the Inner London Education Authority and provided some information on this aspect. The report established that approximately 5 per cent of the school population in the Authority were being provided for in some form of special education outside of the 'normal arrangements of primary and secondary schools'. In order to meet the needs of this 5 per cent of children approximately *13* per cent of the Authority's total teaching force were engaged in some aspect of meeting special educational needs (ILEA, 1985a). The majority of the additional costs of meeting special educational needs relate to the more favourable teaching ratios which usually prevail within special schools, units and classes. In recent years LEAs have been guided in this respect by DES *Circular 4/73*, details of which are shown in table 4.

Circular 4/73 is currently in the process of being revised and replaced by new, and as yet unpublished, guidelines which introduce the idea of a 'statemented' pupil's entitlement to a minimum level of

Table 3: Net recurrent institutional expenditure per full-time equivalent pupil or student — 1983–4 (England).

	Cost Per Pupil/ Student
Nursery Schools	£1230
Primary Schools	£ 730
Secondary Schools	£1015
Special Schools	£3265

Source: DES (1985b) *Statistical Bulletin*, 14/85, London, HMSO

Table 4: DES staffing recommendations for children with special educational needs

Circular 4/73 Recommended Teaching Group Size Per Category of Handicap	
Deaf, Partially Sighted And Speech Defect	6–8
Blind	6
Partially Sighted	9
Maladjusted	7
ESN(M)	11–13
ESN(S)	10
Epileptic	8–10
Physically Handicapped and Delicate	4/5–10
Autistic	6– 8

Source: DES (1973) *Staffing of Special Schools and Classes*, Circular 4/73, London, HMSO

access to a teacher's time. Both 4/73 (and, when it is available, the revised circular) provide guidance to LEAs on the recommended level of resourcing for the '2 per cent' of children with statements of special needs. This guidance operates to produce a highly favourable pupil/teacher ratio in special education in comparison with mainstream primary and secondary schools. For instance, in the years 1983/84 according to DES figures (DES, 1985a) teacher-pupil ratios were as follows:

Table 5: Pupil/Teacher Ratios Within Schools (UK)

Nursery schools	21.7
Primary schools	22.0
Secondary schools	16.0
Special schools	7.0
All schools	17.6

Source: DES (1985a) *Statistical Bulletin*, 13/85, London, HMSO

Whilst pupils with statements receive a relatively rich 'resource diet' in terms both of teaching and non-teaching staff, Warnock's '18 per cent' of children with special needs typically receive a quite different fare. The major responses from LEAs to this group usually comes from its psychological, advisory and special educational support services. The implementation of the 1981 Act has seen both some sizeable expansion and some reorganization of such support services (Gipps and Goldstein, 1984). In addition, special schools operating as 'resource centres' to mainstream schools are increasingly becoming involved in filling the 'resource gap' between the special system and the mainstream system (Dessent, 1984). These support services operate externally to mainstream schools and are usually centrally organized and deployed. Both educational psychologists and special needs advisory and support services are frequently involved in INSET programmes developed by LEAs, to increase the 'awareness' and skills of mainstream teachers. 'Resourcing the 18 per cent', in many LEAs is often closely related to the development and delivery of programmes of this kind. Whatever the merits of both external advisory/support services and INSET, they contrast sharply, in kind and cost, with the provision which is made for pupils who have statements of special needs.

The idea that children at the end of the continuum of need — those with severe and complex special needs — require higher levels of individual attention from teachers would rarely be disputed. That they merit greater entitlement to both teacher time and the available financial resources appears just within a society which expounds humanitarian ideals. Interestingly, as we move further along the continuum of need to children with more moderate difficulties, the issue of resource entitlement can be more controversial. This is particularly the case when it is realized that providing more for this group necessarily entails less for others, for example 'normal' children/'bright' children. However, the disparity in resourcing which exists between children who have statements of special needs and those in mainstream education who are non-statemented, poses enormous problems for the development of non-segregation policies. A resource-based division is effectively imposed, both by DES guidelines and LEA practices, upon the wide variety of special needs found in our schools. *In essence we allocate resources in a discontinuous manner to a continuum of special needs.*

Now, the extent to which children with special needs within an LEA have to be formally assessed, and thereby fall under this separate system of resourcing, depends upon the level of resourcing, and provision which authorities make 'normally available within ordinary schools' (DES, 1983). The analysis and identification of what *is* and more importantly what *should* be normally available for children with special needs in ordinary schools, is critical in the development of LEA policies in this area. Here *no* central guidelines exist. Moreover, there is enormous variability in the amount and quality of mainstream remedial and special needs provision within and between LEAs. The possibility exists for LEAs to develop 'minimal statementing' policies by focussing attention upon the development and extension of what is 'normally available' for children with special needs within mainstream primary and secondary schools. This point will be returned to when the development of alternative resourcing policies is considered.

There are a number of important characteristics of the discontinuity in our present system of resourcing. The system is essentially concerned with resourcing *individual pupils* and *individual needs*. It can be contrasted with approaches to resourcing special needs based upon groups of pupils, 'whole schools' or indeed clusters or groupings of schools. The assumption in our current system seems to be that the existence of special needs cannot be predicted at the level of the school and community but that they occur unpredictably and at random. Of course, many LEAs have developed resource policies which recognize the fact that certain schools, and certain groups of pupils within school, have higher levels of needs than others. Such schools are then usually resourced somewhat differently from other schools within the same authority (for example, ILEA, 1985b). In the case of the Inner London Education Authority substantial numbers of teachers, non-teaching staff and money are distributed to schools on the basis of an educational priority index. In smaller authorities, similar positive discrimination measures may operate, based upon informal, less public and less 'objective' criteria. Interestingly such policies are often seen as being about *social disadvantage* and are unrelated to provision for children with *special educational needs*, in spite of the clear relationships between the two.

There are a number of consequences of this essentially *individual* approach to resourcing. Within this framework, schools can only represent their need for additional resources by 'calling' for formal assessments and statements on *individual* pupils. Here lies the source of much debate, and sometimes acrimony, between LEAs, on the one hand, and mainstream schools and their governing bodies on the other. In the absence of any agreed criteria for what constitutes a special need or upon what should be 'normally available' in ordinary schools, the statement system acts as both definer and means test. Statements effectively determine both sets of criteria. Teachers and parents can come to regard statements as a solution to the difficulties of their children. From the teacher's point of view, statements achieve either much needed new resources within the school or the removal of a demanding special needs pupil to some form of separate provision. For the parent, statements produce a 'guaranteed' measure of special help, otherwise unavailable within the mainstream school, for their child. A behaviourally-oriented observer might be forgiven for viewing such procedures as similar to the learning maze, much loved by animal psychologists. Entering the maze and reaching the end is heavily reinforced!

The second feature of our current individual resource system concerns its separateness from the resourcing of mainstream schools. Most LEAs will have evolved a separate 'special education' budget with its own budget heading, controlled and directed by a separate group of administrative officers. In a large metropolitan authority or shire county, 'special education' may well be centralized so that decisions about the resourcing of mainstream schools are made by locally-based area officers whereas responsibility for special resources are channelled to a centrally-based administrator. In some authorities 'statementing officers' — a new breed of clerical/administrative worker — have appeared on the scene. Divisions of responsibility of this kind may magnify the problem of developing a continuum of resource provision for all children with special needs. In addition, separate sources of LEA resourcing and budgeting are usually 'mirrored' by separatism at the level of schools. Special education teachers are often paid differently — hence the ubiquitous 's' allowances, paid to teachers in special education — but not to others. Such disparities are less of a problem when most special needs teachers work out of sight of their mainstream colleagues in separate special schools. However, bringing special education into mainstream education immediately highlights such differentials and raises questions about their justification. Establishing the accountabilities and responsibilities of special needs teachers in units and special classes within mainstream schools can also be problematic for LEAs. Such staff often find themselves with dual responsibilities (to headteachers of the host school and to LEA special needs advisory staff) and, perhaps, feel they belong to neither. Separation can also occur in terms of the 'ownership' of material resources. Hegarty *et al* (1981) made the following comment concerning the resourcing and funding of integration schemes '. . . If an integration programme is to be fully a part of the school, and pupils with special needs are to take their place alongside peers, this must be reflected in the financial and administrative arrangements as in other ways. If the goal is a single school making differentiated provision for varying needs, then materials and resources must be acquired and held in common by the school as a whole.'

Some Problems for an Alternative Resource Policy

The problems associated with our present *individual* and *separate* system of resourcing children with special needs are clear. Does the solution to resourcing special needs lie in terms of a 'general'/'whole school'/'integrated' method of resourcing schools, as suggested by Sayer (1985)? Such an approach seems to open up exciting, and largely untried, avenues in terms of developing non-segregation approaches. It seems likely, however, that such policies will need to take account of a number of problems. These problems can be clarified by contrasting the view which might be adopted by mainstream schools (headteachers, teachers and governing bodies), with the view, which might be adopted by LEAs (administrators, advisory staff and, perhaps, elected members).

> *School View:* Give us smaller classes and the necessary resources for providing for children with special needs and we will get on with the job of meeting *all* children's needs within ordinary schools.
>
> *LEA View:* How can we be sure that resources allocated to children with special needs will be used to meet their needs and not used for some alternative purposes?

The interplay of views, attitudes and beliefs which underly these two positions are rarely made explicit, but form the very essence of approaches to policy planning and resourcing of special educational needs in Great Britain.

The school view, that the main requirement in order to bring about the integration of children with special needs is for more and better resources, particularly more teachers in ordinary schools is widely held. It is a view which is usually expressed in publications emanating from teacher unions (for example, NUT, 1984). Gross and Gipps (1985) asked mainstream teachers across six LEAs what they required in order to meet special educational needs in ordinary classrooms. The majority view of teachers was that smaller classes were the main requirement. The school view is linked to what appears to be a growing *mistrust* amongst teachers that LEAs may attempt to 'integrate on the cheap'. Sayer (1985) notes,

> Whilst hard pressed teachers in ordinary schools have been made more aware of handicap and the lack of skill or resources to make a response, they have also come to believe that local

authorities are using the mood towards integration in order to cut the expenses of placement in special residential schools, and they look at each case with suspicion and unease, if not hysteria, out of all proportion to the facts or lack of them.

The LEA view is also based upon some *mistrust* — this time of schools. LEA administrators are able to point to examples of the drift of resources away from children with special educational needs in mainstream schools. These are situations where resources originally earmarked for children with special needs are seen to be 'misappropri-ated' and used by headteachers for other purposes. Fears on the part of LEAs that the direction and control of 'special' resources cannot be left solely in the hands of headteachers in ordinary schools are intimately related to the notion of 'protection' in special education. *The need to protect special educational resources underpins the separateness of the current system.* What effectively is being said to schools is, 'Because of the multitude of competing pressures for resources placed upon you, we cannot invest (total) responsibility in you for looking after the in-terests of handicapped and vulnerable children'. These issues come to the fore most clearly when special units are established within ordin-ary schools. Several questions are raised. Who will draw up the job specification for teaching posts? Who will decide upon the composi-tion of the interviewing panel? To whom will teaching staff be re-sponsible? Who directs their work? Rarely will the decisions involved be left solely in the hands of mainstream schools. Arguably, the more that individuals outside of the ordinary school intervene, control and manage such resources, the more likely that both the facilities and the children being served will remain separate from what is considered 'normal', in the context of the school.

Of course the easiest way of ensuring protection of resources for children with special needs is to move the children to a protected establishment — a special school. Within such an establishment special teachers can be paid special salary additions, over and above the remuneration received by their mainstream colleagues. The easiest way of protecting resources *within* the LEA is to develop a separate administrative and advisory system for children with special needs — perhaps even a separate sub-committee of elected members. Thus, for children with special needs, segregation has been the historical corol-lary of protection.

The problems involved here are unlikely to be easily resolved. Both the 'school view' and the 'LEA view' have a strong basis in reality, and it is worth examining why such views exist in the first place. Why is there a school view which is distinct from an LEA view? Are not all parties in an educational service equally concerned to meet the needs of all children? In reality, of course, ordinary schools are not resourced to meet the needs of all the children in their community. In the main they neither regard themselves, nor are they regarded by the LEA, as being responsible for *all* children. Ordinary schools do not 'own' the responsibility for meeting all special educational needs, nor do they 'own' the authority's special resources. They are organized on the assumption that children regarded as 'special' will be catered for elsewhere, and be taught by teachers other than mainstream teachers. A system of resourcing and provision does exist which is separate from the management and resourcing system of ordinary schools. Schools and teachers can always look outside of themselves to this separate system in order to resolve the problems of individual children. When they do look outside, for example to special schools, and see more favourable teaching and resource provision, their perceptions are readily confirmed. In turn, the LEA is *more* accountable to the DES, to HMI, to parents and to the community it serves, for providing for the 'special' child, than it is for the 'normal' child. It is only for the 'special' child that LEAs must 'determine the educational provision to be made' (DES, 1981). LEAs primarily own both the responsibility and the resources for meeting special educational needs. They will, therefore, seek to protect resources for this group rather than others. The issues here are, of course, much wider than resourcing for special needs. They touch upon the relationship between schools and teachers on the one hand and the management and administration of the educational service on the other.

The problem of developing an 'integrated' resource policy for children with special needs is complicated too by the widely differing needs of special children. If we are seriously to look at ways of resourcing ordinary schools to cater for all children, without total reliance upon an individual procedure, then how do we make provision for exceptional needs at the end of the continuum? The resource needs of a multiply handicapped child, a blind or profoundly hearing impaired child may well lay along a special needs continuum. However, the needs of such children can be unique and distinct both in terms of their nature and intensity, and in terms of the educational provision required. Any resource policy would need to take account not only of the continuum of need but also of the discontinuity that exists in the provision required for some 'special needs' children.

An Alternative Approach to Resourcing — Some Possible Directions

A cynical outside observer, surveying the current scene, might be forgiven for concluding that, in the face of *self evident* needs in our schools (i.e. significant numbers of children with learning difficulties requiring additional help or modified arrangements), and at a time of limited and retracting resources, LEAs have evolved a complex obstacle race, which schools and parents must negotiate in order to obtain what they feel is required for the children in their care. Within this set-up, the only additional resources available are spent on the individuals who construct the obstacles in the race — educational psychologists, administrators, 'statementing officers' and additional LEA clerical staff.

Our traditional approach to resourcing special needs has always assumed that special needs are not self evident — that they occur almost at random and need to be discovered and identified by teachers, psychologists and others. Yet the majority group of children with special needs, those who are slow to learn and who pose a range of social/behavioural difficulties, are relatively permanent and *predictable* products of our educational system. An alternative resource policy should build upon this aspect. Such a policy would focus upon the allocation of resources at the level of individual schools or groups of schools rather than individual pupils. John Sayer (1985) comments

> ... There must be a shift from a system which waits for the special needs of individuals to emerge and only then works out a response to them, towards an anticipatory model, in the knowledge that it is the ordinary system which will be called upon ... the aim should be to prevent special needs from arising rather than responding to crisis, to anticipate all needs including those which are made special by not having been anticipated or resourced, and to get on with the job of contributing to the education of the whole community.

How could such an 'anticipatory' or 'predictive' policy operate? One approach might be to literally count the number of children in the locality of any particular school who are thought to have some kind of need for additional resources and to provide resources within the school in advance of the children's arrival. The problem with this approach, quite apart from any difficulties which administrators would have in finding the required resources, is that it still depends upon identifying the special needs of individual pupils. Any resource policy which is based *solely* on the identification of the special needs of individuals is likely to run into the problems which are inherent within our current practices. 'Individual' policies rest upon the notion that needs exist in some kind of absolute fashion — that there is a consensus about what constitutes a need, and that educational difficulties exist only *within* an individual child, rather than arising within the *context* of what schools offer to pupils. In other words such a system would still pose the question of who, in the locality of a school, has special needs? A second approach relates back to the principle of positive discrimination (see chapter 2). This approach is based upon the idea that a resourcing policy for children with special needs in ordinary schools must begin and end with an *explicit* recognition that pupils who are in any way disadvantaged within the educational system merit a disproportionate slice of the overall level of resources. Just as our separate special educational system can be viewed as a particular form of the positive discrimination principle, the same principle could be used to shape resource policies within mainstream education. A local education authority may decide, for instance, to operate a system which makes explicit that 15 per cent of overall staffing and material resources allocated to each secondary school are to be utilized for children with special educational needs. The principle of earmarking and 'protecting' mainstream resources for children with difficulties has its parallel in the special educational system of other countries. In Norway, for instance, 10 per cent of the total staffing resources available are prescribed and allocated to all schools in order to meet special educational needs. Thus, there is a basic allocation of resources for *all* children (including those regarded as special) and an additional allocation for special educational arrangements (Vislie, 1978).

This system of resourcing leaves the questions of who has special needs, and how *many* children have special needs, to individual schools — which is ultimately the only place where these questions can be answered. Such approaches to resourcing are, however, relatively rare in Great Britain. Perhaps the major reason for this is that their introduction, in the absence of any 'new' resources, would involve a redistribution of existing resources within schools and within the educational service — possibly away from the more able and 'average' pupils and from prestigious areas such as sixth-form classes. Few LEAs are prepared to make such an explicit statement regarding the distribution of resources. The interesting feature of the Norwegian approach is that it involves a clear statement, emanating from central government, of positive discrimination in the use of resources. Such a system does not necessarily involve *more* resources — it simply makes a decision about priorities in the use of available resources. An issue more important than the specific details of how such an essentially simple policy would operate, is the question of why such policies are rarely considered by LEAs in Great Britain.

What is being suggested here is that the first step towards the development of an alternative resource policy for children with special needs is to invoke a principle of positive discrimination in the allocation and use of resources within ordinary schools. Such a move would need to apply to *all* schools regardless of catchment area and perceived level of special needs. A policy of this kind would need to stem from a centralized (DES/LEA) initiative, rather than depend upon the decision making of individual schools. However, the nature of its actual operation is likely to depend upon the degrees of consensus in our schools and community about such a principle.

An alternative resource system would also need to consider the issue of positive discrimination *between* schools. Schools clearly differ in terms of a whole host of factors related to social disadvantage, levels of achievement and special educational needs. School A, nestling within the commuter belt of middle-class suburbia, will contrast sharply in these respects with the inner city deprivation of school B. Yet both schools are quite likely to exist in the same authority. Given the close relationship between pupils' socioeconomic background, factors linked to social disadvantage and the incidence of special educational needs, it is quite reasonable to ask the question, 'Should not school B receive a more favourable allocation of resources than school A?' Most LEAs operate an 'informal' resourcing system which recognizes these disparities between schools in terms of both the incidence of disadvantage amongst pupils and the increased pressures on teachers. The Plowden Report (DES, 1967) recommended that priority should be given to schools where educational handicaps were reinforced by social handicaps. Within ILEA such a positive discrimination policy has operated since 1971. The Educational Priority Index in the Inner London Education Authority involves the collection of data '... selected because of their proven relationship to performance in school' (ILEA, 1985). Data are collected anonymously for individual pupils in the following areas:

Eligibility for free meals	Pupils' behaviour
Large families	Pupil mobility
One-parent families	Ethnic family background
Parental occupation	Fluency in English

Combinations of these factors carry a particular measurable risk of educational disadvantage. Via questionnaire returns from schools, pupils are assigned a weighting reflecting the measures on which they score. An Educational Priority Index score is then calculated for each school, based upon the sum of the 'weights' of individual pupils. Index scores are used in the allocation of quite considerable staffing and financial resources to schools — resources which have been separated out and held back from the authority's basic resourcing system for normal primary and secondary schools. Thus in ILEA, an individual primary school established as having high priority needs might be allocated several more full time teachers and substantially greater cash input than an equivalent sized school with a more favourable 'catchment area'. This represents a resourcing system which is based upon individually assessed needs but which operates at the level of the school rather than at the level of the individual child.

Interestingly, such positive discrimination policies are rarely seen as having anything to do with special educational needs. If they operate at all, they do so alongside, and without regard to, a separate individually based special education system. In practice, a school could be allocated considerable additional resources related to their priority rating. The same school could then 'refer out' a sizeable number of individual children to a separately resourced special system. Yet the close relationship between ILEA's indicators of needs and the educational performance and behavioural difficulties experienced by individual pupils have been clearly established, both within mainstream schools (ILEA, 1982) and special schools (ILEA, 1984b). Perhaps the linking together of such resource policies, which allocate differential resources to schools, with the idea of meeting a school's *special educational needs,* merits careful consideration in the future.

'Whole school', as opposed to individually-based, approaches to resourcing special needs will need to be supplemented and elaborated in a number of ways, if they are to be effective in achieving non-segregation approaches to meeting special needs. Earmarking a certain level of resources for children with special needs will not, of itself, solve the problems which LEAs and schools currently face in this area. The organization, deployment and use of resources within schools needs to be worked out between ordinary schools and the LEA's advisory and support services, to ensure that positive discrimination is more than just a 'paper principle'. It must have a reality as far as individual pupils are concerned. Whole-school resource policies are only likely to be effective within agreed guidelines and principles. One such principle might be that priority within schools should go to the children with the greatest needs. Such a principle could counteract the problems previously noted of 'resource drift'. Thus *the* individual pupil with the greatest level of perceived need becomes the pupil with the greatest claim on available resources. Such a principle will be controversial in terms of its practical operation. At the extreme it could entail one pupil consuming all of the available resource. Nevertheless, it would serve to counteract situations where the available provision is diluted to cover a large number of pupils in a school. The result is, usually, that those children with the most needs are referred for additional support outside of the school.

The idea of 'protection', and the safeguarding of 'special' resources, cannot wholly be overcome given the social and political context within which special education operates. A system geared towards resourcing schools, or clusters of schools within an area, rather than 'statemented' individuals will need an inbuilt system of monitoring. In this respect an LEA's psychological and advisory service would have an important role to play (see chapter 6). Support services would operate to monitor and evaluate the use of resources for children with special needs within ordinary schools. A contractual system could be envisaged between ordinary schools and the LEA. Within such a system, ordinary schools would, in conjunction with support services develop proposals for the deployment of their 'special' resources, as a response to the needs of the children in their school. Once agreed and put into operation such schemes would be subject to monitoring, evaluation and subsequent modification. Individual pupils 'referred' by schools as requiring additional resources would (as now) be looked at in terms of the schools' existing resources and ability to meet needs. However, unlike the current situation, this would occur within a framework where schools were accountable for priority allocations of their resources to children with special needs and, within this framework, to those children with the *greatest* needs. Within such a system LEAs, and schools could begin to define what should be 'normally available' in ordinary schools.

What of the situation with regard to exceptional needs? While a whole school resource policy may go a long way towards promoting the development of provision for the majority of children with educational difficulties, it is unlikely to be able to cater for individual pupils with relatively rare and unpredictable special needs. Children with multiple handicaps, and children with severe visual, hearing and/or physical handicaps, are still likely to require an individual approach to resourcing their needs. In the Norwegian system the majority needs are catered for by the '10 per cent principle', and these resources are known as the 'A' funds. Individual handicapped children are provided for via 'B' funds, which in Norway are refunded by central government to their county administration following an assessment by an educational psychologist. Is this not reminiscent of the 1981 Act, or 'statementing revisited'!? Inevitably, this additional layer of resourcing retains many of the problems of an individual system. Booth (1982), commenting on the Norwegian 'B' fund approach, notes that,

> Although such procedures are a financial safeguard for the handicapped, they do induce teachers to differentiate between normal and handicapped children. It is envisaged that at some point during the gradual integration now happening, such separate categories and funding will no longer be necessary. That will be the point at which schools share out resources naturally according to need.

In whatever way an individual resource system operated it would require a form of *definition* to avoid the worst abuses of our current system. It would need to operate so as to minimize the number of children regarded by schools as 'special' in the sense of requiring 'special resources'. Norman Tutt (1985) has made the point that the concept of 'special educational needs' is of little use in this context. '. . . Whilst the concept of needs may be useful in terms of professional discussion, it is totally inappropriate, inadequate and detrimental when allied to the bureaucratic structures of service delivery . . .'. Any form of definition or criterion for additional special funds will be open to debate and also to potential abuse. Administrators, psychologists and LEA advisers usually give a less than precise answer to the question, 'What are the criteria operating for formal assessment and statementing in your authority?' Newly trained arrivals to LEA psychological services often struggle greatly with these issues because of the absence of any explicit criteria. Clearly, though, criteria do operate in LEAs, although as Tutt notes in his article '. . . professional consensus on special educational needs is very weak'. Perhaps individual approaches to resourcing special needs, which are supplementary to a general resource policy, should develop around concepts such as 'disability' and 'life long needs'. Within this context the concern would be with disabled and handicapped children, whose existence could not readily be predicted at the level of individual schools or groupings of schools, and whose needs for additional resources were less likely to be the subject of debate and disagreement. For such children the terms 'physical', 'sensory' or 'mental handicap' could be used without undue ambiguity. Realistically, in any resource policy for children with special needs, we have to accept a continuing need for mechanisms of control and monitoring, linked to both the protection issue and to some form of individualized resourcing. The main thrust however would be the development of policies which *reduce to a minimum the need for resources linked to individual pupils.* This contrasts sharply with current LEA practices, where there appears to be an increasing number of pupils who are being picked out, made 'special' in some way, and who become the subject of statements in order to procure additional resources.

Comment

The main focus of this chapter has been on the development of alternative approaches to resourcing children with special needs, in order to promote better provision within mainstream primary and secondary schools. The view has been taken that resource approaches which depend totally upon the identification of the needs of individual pupils are less than helpful in this respect. Instead, resourcing schemes need to be developed at the level of schools, or of clusters of schools. Such schemes would need to be based upon an explicit principle of positive discrimination in the use and deployment of resources to those children with the greatest perceived needs. Such policies would probably entail differential resourcing between schools based upon differences in the child population being served. Individual resource approaches would supplement these policies for a small number of pupils with serious disabilities. The result would be a reduction in the number of children who were 'statemented', 'ascertained' or individually resourced in some way. A concern to reduce the number of individual statements in an LEA should not, as some writers have suggested, for example Newell (1985), be inevitably linked to the motive of saving money. So called 'minimal statementing' policies can only make educational sense within a context of either additional resourcing or a redistribution of existing resources in favour of children with special needs.

Chapter 6

Support Services and the Nature of Special Expertise

A few LEAs have appointed teachers with special qualifications to visit a group of schools ... to help and advise upon
the treatment of backward children. As an interim measure,
until teachers in general have gained a greater knowledge of
the educational needs of backward children, this practice has
its value, but the creation of a new class of specialist peripatetic
teachers as a permanency would be as likely to hinder as to
help the spread of knowledge and skill in handling backward
children, because of the temptation that would beset the
teachers in the schools to depend upon such outside help rather
than on their own resources. *The Education of Backward Children* (1937) Board of Education pamphlet, p. 112.

'When we talk about meeting special educational needs in ordinary
schools, the word *support* should be eradicated from our vocabulary'.
This was the view expressed by a headteacher of a large comprehensive school during a discussion about the role of special needs support
services. The opinion of this head was that support services — educational psychologists, and the range of peripatetic/advisory teachers —
had proved generally unhelpful to ordinary schools in the task of
meeting special educational needs. His views may not be representative of those of the majority of headteachers. Nevertheless, it would
be difficult to sustain the argument that external support services to
ordinary schools have been an unqualified success. On the other hand
an increasing number of mainstream schools are calling for more and
better support for children with special educational needs. In the wake
of the 1981 Act and the new responsibilities which have been placed
on ordinary schools, the question of how the so-called '18 per cent'
can be supported in mainstream schools, has been brought sharply

into focus. The major resource inputs made by LEAs to the '18 per cent' come in the form of external support services and the inservice training of mainstream teachers (see chapter 5). The staffing of school psychological services is almost universally being increased. Peripatetic remedial services and a whole range of advisory teaching services have undergone rapid reorganization and change in order to deal with the so-called 'implications of the Act' (Gipps and Goldstein, 1984). New support service names abound: SENS (Special Educational Needs Service), SEAS (Special Educational Advisory Service), and SNAS (Special Needs Advisory Service) are some of the latest labels being used in the field of support. Gipps and Gross (1984) list thirty-eight different names for support services in their study. Special schools, with an uneasy eye on their roles, are also getting in on the 'support' act, utilizing the concept of a special school acting as a resource centre (Dessent, 1984). It seems likely that educational administrators will regard such support services as an increasingly vital part of a local authority's provision for children with special needs, in that they provide one method of meeting their authority's statutory responsibilities under the Act. Yet, despite the moderate build-up and restructuring of a range of so-called support services for children with special needs, there is no available evidence to indicate that support services meet the very obvious needs of ordinary schools. Nor is it clear that they are effective in meeting one of their commonly stated aims — to meet children's special needs within the mainstream and thereby avoid the need for special educational placement. The data provided by Goodwin (1983) indicates that, if anything, quite the reverse is true, and that *increasing the availability of support services can increase the likelihood of segregated provision being made for children with special needs.*

If we ask the question, 'How do we support children with special needs in ordinary schools?', the honest answer is, that at the present time, we do not know how. It is likely that the newly-organized support services which are emerging and the precious few new posts which LEAs can make available, will lead to more of the same. There is a need to learn from what has happened thus far, in order that the wheels on which educational psychologists, remedial and advisory teachers are still spinning around, are not reinvented.

The focus of this chapter will be upon the services which have traditionally formed·the LEA's response to supporting children with special needs in ordinary schools — educational psychologists and remedial/special peripatetic and advisory services. Firstly, a critique will be offered of support services as they have traditionally operated. Secondly, it will be suggested that support services have floundered because of a failure to address certain crucial issues in the field of special educational needs. A view will then be put forward suggesting some possible future directions for the work of support services. Finally, attention will be focussed upon the nature of 'expertise' in special education, an issue which is linked to both the work of support services and to INSET and training in special education.

Support Services for Children with Special Needs — A Critical Analysis

Most educational support services in the field of special needs tend to evolve broadly similar structures and patterns of working to cope with the demands placed upon them. This is particularly the case with services which relate to the great majority of children with special needs — those with learning difficulties. There are obvious problems in generalizing about such a varied field of work. Nevertheless, the following are some common features of support services as they have traditionally operated.

Individual / Referral Orientated

In the main, ordinary schools refer *individual* children to support services. The emphasis, therefore is usually upon special needs residing within the individual child — a model of special needs based firmly upon individual deviance. This model operates within a context where awareness of the importance of curriculum, teaching methods, teacher attitudes and school ethos in defining and engendering special needs is growing. Such factors are usually not the subject of referral to support services although increasing emphasis is being placed upon the development of 'whole school' policies by some advisory services. Because individual children are the main focus of support services most will, almost by definition, be seen as 'thin on the ground', overworked and plagued by inevitable waiting lists. Ordinary schools are very familiar with these facts, particularly as it relates to school psychological services and most will react with some surprise if an early response is made to a referral! The process of referral — particularly those more elaborate systems which referral agencies evolve — is an understandable response on the part of the 'thin on the ground' support service to cope with the overwhelming demands that could be placed upon them by mainstream schools.

The consequences of having a support service which requires a referral system are worth highlighting. If the referral process is lengthy and bureaucratic it is likely that any intervention on the part of the support service will come later, rather than sooner, in the evolution of the 'referred problem'. In other words, crisis intervention becomes the rule rather than the exception. The prevailing attitudes of teaching staff, headteacher and parents to the 'problem' are likely to differ significantly when this is the case. It is easy to forget that most referrals of children with special needs already have a lengthy 'social and political' history by the time the referral forms reach their destination on the desk of the educational psychologist, advisory teacher or remedial teacher. The child's difficulties may have been discussed for several years between teachers and parents with the often inevitable feelings of anxiety and guilt, which frequently surround educational failure, now being linked to the problem. By the time the support agency arrives on the scene the referrers have often already 'decided' exactly what should now happen to the child. Frequently, this will entail a 'decision' that the child certainly requires help which they (the normal school) cannot provide and a consequent decrease in their feelings of responsibility for the child's difficulties. Perhaps the school is no longer prepared to make any internal/organizational/resource changes to meet the child's needs. The support service's task is now further complicated. How does the service go about supporting a school or a teacher who does not want their form of support? If a referral system is an open one, then inevitably, support services will spend a significant amount of their time responding to, and attempting to support, schools and mainstream teachers, some of whom do not really want the support that is being offered. In fact, most support agencies evolve a pattern of working which often, by quite subtle methods, tends to avoid contact with certain schools which react negatively to support. Instead, they concentrate their efforts on the 'good' schools which react positively.

Referral to an 'Expert'

Most support services in education involve the referral of 'problem' children to individuals who are regarded as experts. Frequently, intervention is of a one-off nature, and, as a general rule, there is a limited amount of contact between the expert and those involved in the problem situation (i.e., the classroom teacher). Perhaps the days have gone when the educational psychologist only ever saw the child and the headteacher or when the remedial specialist's visit consisted only of the customary 20 minutes in a drafty corridor with a failing reader, both to the exclusion of contact with the classroom teacher. However, it is questionable whether any educational support service has really satisfactorily resolved the problem of adequate liaison and communication with the 'significant others' in the child's educational life.

Being an expert has a number of other unfortunate consequences. Expectations on the part of the referrer as to what the expert can do can be exceedingly high and can, perhaps, rarely be met. This in turn can lead to 'maladaptive' behaviour on the part of the expert who is often under extreme pressure to demonstrate his/her expertise. Experts in education can find themselves engaging in practices and behaviours in which they have little faith or belief but which serve the purpose of meeting the expectations of those they are attempting to advise. Diagnostic testing, 'within-child' labelling and initiating special educational placements can be examples of 'maladaptive behaviours' from so-called experts.

Educational psychologists are daily confronted by the problems associated with the expert syndrome. Take, for instance, the problem of responding to the individual pupil referred from a mainstream school which is itself inadequately resourced to meet the child's special needs. Perhaps the teaching staff no longer have the energy or the inclination to work at the individual child's problems. How does the psychologist respond to such a situation? The all too frequent cry from mainstream staff is that, 'something must be done'. Often the educational psychologist is left feeling that he/she can only respond, with any credibility, by 'pushing the special educational placement button'.

Does a comprehensive support service to mainstream schools need to rest upon the kind of expert service which advisory teachers and psychologists have provided in the past? Learning difficulties are a permanent phenomenon of our current educational system. They tend to be persistent also at the level of the individual child. They do not easily and readily disappear following a quick word of advice from a remedial/psychological 'expert'. *The children need a continuous and maintained system of help in their learning*, often throughout their school careers. Whatever role is played in future by 'thin on the ground' experts in terms of supporting these children, one can be certain that the traditional system of referral and assessment followed by limited, or one-off, intervention will continue to be totally inadequate on its own. What both the children with learning difficulties and their teachers require, is immediate access to resources, materials and advice at an early stage in the recognition of the problem, from a colleague who is close at hand.

Definers of 'Specialness' and 'Resourceworthiness'

The employment by LEAs of special needs support personnel, and particularly educational psychologists, is intimately linked to their role as definers of 'specialness' and definers of 'resourceworthiness'. While, ostensibly, ordinary schools refer to such agencies for 'advice' and 'support', there is a clear but unwritten agenda which underpins referral. Within this unwritten agenda ordinary schools first look to support services to 'validate' that an individual child is exceptional or special in some way. Secondly, they may, in some cases, look to the support service to remove the responsibility for resourcing and educating an individual child from the ordinary school ...

> A central feature of the educational psychologist's role in special education is the job of *defining responsibility* for special educational needs. His/her local authority employers, and indeed schools themselves, may care little about the detail of the assessment and diagnostic procedures used so long as this central administrative role in special education is performed. The vast majority of referrals to an educational psychologist can be regarded as questions along the lines of: 'Is this child our responsibility or somebody else's?' (special school, remedial services, child guidance, etc). Psychologists in most areas could easily list 'good' and 'bad' schools in terms of the school's ability to cater for children with special needs. 'Good' schools are identified by the fact that the head and class teachers within the school assume personal and professional responsibility for teaching *all* children in their area rather than by the possession of any particular technical expertise, teaching approaches or methods of organization. Such schools require dramatically less involvement from psychologists as definers of special needs. School psychological services and related services (child guidance, child psychiatry) have a built in survival mechanism by virtue of their role as definers and sharers

of responsibility for special needs children. One quickly becomes aware as a psychologist that by simply visiting the
school and talking to or listening to the teacher of a referred
child you are often regarded as providing a useful service
because in so doing the responsibility for the child is shared
with you and often imperceptibly transferred to you! (Dessent,
1983).

The link which educational psychologists, in particular, have to
the formal legislative procedures leading to 'statementing' and thus to
obtaining different or additional resources for children with special
needs, places them in a weak position to genuinely support individual
pupils in the mainstream. Schools are in the situation of having to
'persuade' the psychologist that the child's problems really are significant and serious and therefore not readily solved by minor changes
in teaching approaches. Support services are likely, even within an
alternative resourcing system for children with special needs, to be
involved, to some extent, in 'the definition game' (see chapter 5).
However, what is being suggested here, is that providing genuine
support to mainstream teachers will always be undermined where a
support service is predominantly linked to resource allocation procedures for individual children.

High Priority to Assessment and Diagnosis

Experts in the field of special needs have been obsessed with the need
for assessment and diagnosis. A popular maxim within educational
psychology and remedial education has been — 'no remediation
without assessment and no assessment without remediation'. Support
services have become accomplished at the business of assessment but
most remain novices when it comes to remediation and intervention.
Assessment is the easy part of the process; intervention, particularly
when this involves finding ways round the organizational problems of
schools which frequently seem to be producing or exacerbating the
problems of individual pupils, is usually more difficult. So too are the
problems involved in finding individual or small group teaching time
for pupils with learning difficulties. Most referrals to support services
for children with learning difficulties emanate from the school's inability to find time, within their organizational and resource constraints, to meet the children's needs for individualized or small group
teaching.

Arguably, far too much time has been spent by support services on the assessment of individual pupils, to the neglect of issues related to intervention. How many of the pupils referred really *do* require a detailed psychometric assessment in order for appropriate intervention to be organized? Is it not simply that many mainstream schools have insufficient resources and inadequate materials available to meet the needs of individual pupils? This, coupled with the fact that so few schools have their own internal system for monitoring, discussing and planning teaching approaches for children with special needs, are the major reasons underlying referral. Yet, the raison d'être of so many support services has been built on the need to help schools, and ordinary classroom teachers, to identify and properly assess their pupils. Most teachers really do not need help in identifying which of their pupils have special needs. Most commercial tests and check lists which have been produced for the purpose of identifying and screening pupils with special needs, ultimately, depend for their validity on teacher judgments and opinions. While there are variations between class teachers in their perceptions of pupils with special needs, this should not cloud the truth of the matter, which is that mainstream teachers have a very clear idea of which pupils are struggling and, within the context of their schools, those who require additional support. Often, if the records of failing pupils are traced back far enough, one finds that the identification of the pupil's learning difficulties occurred early in the infant years by the child's first class teacher. What prevents the more explicit identification and assessment of pupils with special needs in schools is not the absence of expertise in diagnostic assessment skills, but the non-availability of provision within schools to meet these needs. It is a familiar finding in most LEAs that once a specialist facility or service arrives (for example, special school, special unit), few mainstream schools have problems in identifying and assessing more than enough pupils to fill the establishment! What mainstream schools require are not more services from expert testers and assessors, but adequate forms of providing for pupils within their schools. By placing the emphasis of support services on providing assessment and advice, LEAs may be creating a (perhaps understandable) administrative/political smokescreen, to avoid the issue of *adequate provision* for pupils with special needs. Increasing the ranks of the expert assessors (whether they be educational psychologists or specialist teachers), may have the affect of simply increasing the number of individuals who can validate what the schools already know, i.e., that many schools are poorly organized and resourced to meet the needs of individual pupils with difficulties.

The implications of all this for support services would be that their focus needs to be much more upon helping schools to organize their own intervention and resources to meet the needs of individual pupils, rather than upon the assessment and diagnosis of individual pupils' difficulties.

No Requirement for Resource / Organizational Change Within the School

Consider traditional support services at their best. Perhaps as a result of responding to a number of individual referrals over an extended period of time from a mainstream school, and establishing good working relationships with staff and headteacher, significant organizational and attitudinal changes occur within the school being supported. For example, the school allocates a competent teacher and a post of responsibility to 'children with special needs'; the head allocates a significant proportion of capitation to purchase learning resources, and staff eagerly respond to INSET courses in the field of special needs. Perhaps, in addition, the school produces a written policy for identifying, assessing and providing for children with special needs, and has a comprehensive scheme involving the parents of children with learning difficulties in their child's reading development. Partly, perhaps, because this occurs so infrequently it sounds like Utopia! The important point is that these kinds of organizational changes are rarely built into an LEA's modus operandi for either its mainstream schools or its support services. Yet, if we accept that the majority of children with special needs, particularly those with learning problems, are likely to have some long-term educational difficulties, then the children concerned require a maintained and continuous form of help. This can only be provided in any realistic way if schools have their own internal, organizational system for responding to the needs of individual special needs pupils. Such a system is certain to involve either additional resources from the LEA or some realignment or reallocation of resources within a school in the direction of children with special need. However, the way in which most support services are currently organized and administered means that they need to respond to referrals from all schools regardless of the school's motivation to help themselves in supporting children with special needs.

Thus, there is little recognition of a central aspect of the whole business of 'support' — that it can only be effective if both parties, the provider and the recipient, are prepared to make a commitment to resolving and managing problems.

At risk of overgeneralizing, an outline has been presented of some of the characteristics and difficulties faced by traditional support services in the field of special needs. In view of the framework and the constraints within which such services operate, they not surprisingly tend to have a bad press. The consumers (in this case teachers within ordinary schools) often appear dissatisfied with the service which they receive (Gross and Gipps, 1985). In addition, it is not at all clear that external support services are successful in increasing the ability of ordinary schools to cater for children with special needs. There is the possibility that increasing the number of support service personnel who operate externally to ordinary schools will, in turn, increase the likelihood of segregated provision being made for children with special needs. Perhaps, the very process of providing support is itself a step on the path to segregated education. 'Special support' is not provided to all pupils. It is something that is applied (or supplied) to a minority group. This minority group has to first be identified, recorded, referred and assessed. Then decisions have to be made about them. All of these can be seen as steps which progressively validate the individual pupil's dissimilarities to other so-called 'normal' pupils. If the pupil is then referred to a support service which offers something to which the referring body cannot readily respond, (for example, detailed assessment and 'impractical advice'), then the child's educational failure is further compounded — in the first instance by the school's failure to respond to the child's needs, and in the second, by the support service's failure to respond to the needs of the school. The process ends with the support service initiating procedures leading to special educational placement. If this is a valid description of what is currently happening between pupils / schools and support services, then we might anticipate that the recent moderate increases in the number of educational psychologists and other support services may lead to increases both in the number of formal assessments carried out by LEAs and in the number of children singled out in some way, 'statemented' and labelled as special. There are some indications that this is exactly what is happening nationally in the case of children with learning difficulties (Swann, 1985).

The trend towards converting special schools into the Warnock concept of 'resource centres', so that an advisory teaching service can be offered to pupils in mainstream schools, will need to be closely monitored for the same possible effects. The so-called 'vacuum cleaner' phenomenon may occur, i.e., special school staff will identify large numbers of pupils who can, as a result of the 'failure' of mainstream intervention, be demonstrated to require the provision of a separate special school. Children will thereby be 'sucked-up' into the segregated system.

There is as yet no clear evidence as to whether support systems inadvertently have the effect of increasing the incidence of segregated provision. There are, however, enough indications, to lead LEAs to exercise caution when considering increasing the level of support services *external to ordinary schools themselves*. Certainly, some clear thinking should precede such increases. Particular thought needs to be given to how such increases are likely to influence mainstream schools in improving their *own* ability to provide for children with special needs. We might anticipate that the greater the build up of external support services (to the neglect of provision within schools), the more difficult will be the task of persuading mainstream schools to retain responsibility for teaching children with special needs.

Support Services-Addressing the Issues

Support services have not been unaware of the range of difficulties which they confront within a changed and evolving framework of meeting special educational needs. Within the ranks of educational psychologists there has been much heart searching concerning roles. There has been a concern to identify what is the unique contribution of educational and child psychologists and attempts to 'reconstruct' educational psychology (e.g., Gillham, 1978; Norwich, 1983). Few professional groups could have spent so much time and energy agonizing over such issues and to have resolved so little in practice. Similarly, the allied field of remedial education has, for at least as long as educational psychology, entertained the need to 'reconstruct' the role of remedial teachers (NARE, 1979; Golby and Gulliver 1979; Smith, 1985).

It would be fair to say that these 'reconstructing' movements, aimed at developing new roles for psychological, special and remedial support staff, have clarified the nature of the problems confronted by such services. However, what is frequently advocated is a series of desirable but largely unrealizable new roles for psychologists and special/remedial teachers. The view often taken is that educational psychologists should 'give psychology away', act as consultants, innovators and instigators of new projects, in-service educators etc. Similarly, remedial teachers should act as 'consultants' to their subject colleagues, spread their expertise across the curriculum and become an agent of curriculum and institutional change. What is suggested here is that the major problem for such services is not what they *should* do but how LEAs and schools are going to function if they stopped doing what they are doing now. Support services have failed to address the major issues which underpin their current roles.

The Resource Issue

The reconstructing movement in educational psychology singularly failed to confront the issue of how LEAs could resource and provide for children with special needs without recourse to educational psychologists as definers of 'resourceworthiness'. Since this role is the main reason why LEAs employ educational psychologists, this is perhaps not surprising! It remains to be seen whether large numbers of educational psychologists would be employed if they were no longer required to carry out this defining role. What is clear, however, is that no amount of 'reconstructing' of roles and no amount of exhortation to educational psychologists that they should be 'doing something different' is likely to lead anywhere positive in the long run until the *issue of resources* and the educational psychologist's role as an LEA definer of 'resourceworthiness' is tackled. The defining role expected by the LEA produces related expectations from schools, parents and allied professional groups. This further obstructs the development of alternative roles and methods of working. Moreover, it is likely that the movement into a tripartite system (school, doctors and educational psychologists) of assessing and defining needs under the 1981 Act assessment procedures will increase, rather than decrease, the psychologist's role problem. Under the 1981 Act procedures, educational psychologists are firmly nailed and fastened as 'assessors and definers' of needs and resources. They are likely to find themselves seeing and assessing an ever increasing number of individual children for whom they will produce something called 'psychological advice'. Yet, how many children seen by educational psychologists actually require psychological assessment or psychological advice? With the demise in popularity of normative, 'closed' psychometric testing, many educational psychologists are embarrassed by the question — 'What is psychological advice?'. Arguably, the vast majority of children seen by educational psychologists have need of *purely educational* and *teaching* resources —

small teaching groups, individualized help, modified curriculum and modified teaching methods. They do not require psychological assessment, nor indeed do they primarily require a heavy dose of behavioural objectives, precision teaching or a behaviour modification programme. *Children who are slow to learn and who pose a range of social/ behavioural difficulties are relatively permanent products of our educational system. They will not go away without a radical reconstruction of what education is seen to be about.* Such children are proffered up as requiring multidisciplinary assessment, psychological assessment and advice so that LEAs may control access to scarce resources. Educational psychologists have always performed a social regulation role. Now the economic realities of the 1970s and 1980s have involved them increasingly in a form of economic regulation within the education service.

What is suggested here is that the *resource issue* both underpins and undermines the role of educational psychologists as a support service to mainstream schools. Educational psychologists are not alone in this respect. The gathering armies of new special education support teachers will confront the same issue. The development of a large, centralized special needs support service is an obvious answer for LEAs confronted by a massive, and ultimately indefinable, resourcing problem. Putting all their special resources for mainstream schools into a central team, out of the hands and control of ordinary schools, is the cheapest possible way of defining what resources should be made available to meet special needs in ordinary schools. Disenchantment with educational psychologists as 'supporters' is likely to give way to disenchantment with the new breed of specialist support teacher services. Only within the context of a resourcing and management policy (see chapters 3 and 5), which attempts to match the continuum of special need with a continuity of resourcing, can external support services begin the attempt to 'support' teachers and children with special needs in ordinary schools. Within such a context, support services would be working 'beyond the resources issue'. An attempt could then be made to work with the resource and organizational structures of mainstream schools on an intervention model rather than a definition model.

The 'Expertise' Issue

What is the expertise possessed by 'special' educators? What expertise would support services be delivering to mainstream schools in their attempt to support children with special needs? What should INSET training in special educational needs consist of? The expert-oriented nature of most support services has already received comment. Being perceived as an 'expert' can undermine attempts to provide support. This still, however, begs the question of what specific service a psychological or special educational advisory teacher is attempting to deliver in the support role. The historical separation of special education from mainstream education has provided a breeding ground for the development of a range of myths concerning the 'expertise' possessed by special educators. Mainstream teachers may, for instance, come to believe that their special colleagues are a particular 'breed' of teacher in terms of personal skills, tolerance and commitment to the disadvantaged — veritable paragons of virtue! Further, that they possess a range of specific qualifications and training which confers upon them exclusive skills in assessment, teaching methods and therapeutic education. To some extent these beliefs are important to mainstream staff to hold regardless of their validity. A belief that something better, someone with more expertise exists in the special school acts to justify the continued exclusion of pupils from mainstream schools. Advisers and educational psychologists working between mainstream and special education, quickly become aware that myths of this kind have little or no basis in reality. Yet the view is often expressed that the integration of children with special needs must wait upon the retraining of all ordinary school teachers. Mainstream staff are seen as needing to acquire a form of special expertise. This view is at best simplistic and at worst fundamentally misguided.

As special education progressively moves its location into mainstream schools, the vast overlap and common ground which exists between mainstream and special education teachers becomes clearer. Outside of special schools for children with visual and hearing impairments, only about one-fifth of teachers working in special schools have a specialist qualification. Of course, for hearing and visually impaired children who have severe and profound handicaps — as well as a minority of children requiring alternative, non-oral communication methods — we can identify specific and exclusive areas of skill and expertise. Teaching a blind child to use braille requires something more than a sympathetic 'generalist' who has attended a special needs awareness course! However, when we attempt to analyze the skills, expertise and knowledge of teachers working with the majority group of children with special needs, little can be found which is exclusive to either the teachers or children concerned. Sayer (1985) comments '... the skills and qualities required to meet most of the needs described as special, are those which are desirable in any good teacher for any pupils'. Yet, within this context the idea of support services operating to 'advise', 'train' and 'raise the level of expertise' of mainstream teachers has developed. Support services which operate on this model with 'special expertise' writ large are probably doomed to failure. *They fail to recognize both the communality of skills and expertise between the 'special' and the 'normal' and the fact that successful support is a two-way process. It occurs at its best when the resolution of problems is seen as a mutual and shared conern.*

To recognize the similarities and communalities between the mainstream and the special implies no denigration of the skills and commitment of teachers within special education, of educational psychologists or of other support service personnel. Differences of emphasis and experience do exist. Many mainstream teachers move into special education because their attitudes and personal qualities appear more congruent with a 'child centred' (rather than 'subject centred') approach. Personal qualities such as tolerance for diversity, a concern for the disadvantaged, and acceptance of the rights and dignity of the handicapped, are crucial. They are not, however, qualities exclusive to teachers working in the special field. The experiences of teachers who enter special education will usually lead towards the development of more *individualized* approaches to teaching and learning. Teaching children in smaller teaching groups enables all teachers to *individualize* their teaching. Individualizing education essentially involves close attention being paid to the following three elements:

(i)   A knowledge and awareness of the characteristics, needs and difficulties of an individual child (identification and assessment).

(ii)   An ability to find and establish realistic teaching objects (goal planning).

(iii) The development and implementation of differentiated teaching materials and methods (intervention).

Now it is clear that if special expertise is linked to an increased ability to individualize education, then the skills and qualities required are desirable for *all* teachers and *all* children. All children need to have their needs identified, realistic goals set for their education and an educational programme matched to needs and objectives. Special expertise is simply an extension of the expertise of all teachers. For instance, skills of task analysis and the establishment of optimal learning conditions are an inherent feature of all successful teaching. Teachers in special education simply have a greater opportunity to do this than do most of their mainstream colleagues. Moreover, they are more likely subsequently to seek out training opportunities which will further equip them to develop individualized approaches to programme planning.

Skills in individualized education may form the core of what is meant by 'special expertise'. However, it cannot be assumed that the individualizing skills of remedial and special educators are entirely relevant, outside of the particular learning environments of special schools and special units. For instance, the skills in individualizing subject-based curricula in a secondary school, or topic/project work in the primary school, are only likely to come from teachers who know about the teaching of, say, science, geography and history in the secondary school, or topic and project work in the primary school. Remedial and special educators may have a contribution to make in terms of methodology but are unlikely to possess all of the necessary skills. The consequences of recognizing the non-exclusive nature of expertise for INSET training within LEAs, university departments and institutes of higher education have, as yet, barely begun to be recognized.

What are the implications, for external support services to ordinary schools, of this particular view of special expertise? Firstly, it must imply that support services, whether they stem from educational psychologists or specialist teachers, need to emphasise that mainstream teachers do, in the main, possess the skills and expertise necessary to meet the majority of special needs. Moreover, that children with special needs require 'good' teaching rather than 'special' teaching. This entails a model of service delivery which de-emphasizes 'mystical' assessment and therapeutic procedures based upon the idea of exclusive expertise. Instead, we need a model in which individuals work together, as mutual resources to each other, to resolve shared problems. Secondly, we are led to a view which stresses that the primary requirement for mainstream teachers is that they have greater *opportunity* to develop individualized approaches to educating their pupils with special needs. Skills in individualizing education can be enhanced by attending a training course but they rest essentially upon an opportunity to develop and employ such skills in daily teaching experiences. This would entail an increased opportunity for all teachers to work with the children concerned in small group or individual situations, and returns us, of course, to the primacy of the resource issue. Ordinary schools require flexibility in their staffing in order that teachers can direct their energies towards individualized curriculum and courses. By *first* providing mainstream teachers with an increased opportunity to individualize their approaches to children with special needs, we would be in a clearer position to determine what additional skills and expertise would be required from support services and in-service education. All three aspects of individualized education listed above are likely to be important. However, perhaps the development of realistic teaching objectives is most critical. Expectations amongst mainstream teachers concerning the progress which it is possible for some children to make in their learning can be exceedingly high. *Expertise in special education is sometimes more to do with knowing what cannot be done than with knowing what can be done.* Living with educational failure and making appropriate curricular and teaching adjustments to re-define what counts as 'success' is probably, at the end of the day, what expertise in special education is really about.

The 'Failure' Issue

Support services to ordinary schools have rarely addressed the issue of educational failure. They have traditionally operated on a 'success' or 'curative' model. Their job being construed as delivering their expertise to mainstream staff in assessment, in teaching methods or in programme planning in order to 'normalize' the individual failing child. The development of 'objectives based' approaches to curriculum planning (for example, Ainscow and Tweddle, 1979), of precision teaching (Raybould and Solity, 1985) and of behaviourally based approaches to intervention, place particular emphasis on 'success' and 'normalization'. Few people would want to argue that maximizing educational success and maximizing the learning of basic skills and the attainment of academic goals were not desirable for children with special educational needs. However, the suggestion here is that 'success models' in special education are fraught with problems.

If children with special needs are to be educated appropriately within mainstream education then a major requirement must be that mainstream teachers learn to live with the *relative* 'failure' of pupils in traditional educational skills. Education is about change, progress and learning. Yet the knowledge that teachers in ordinary schools need to acquire is that progress and learning can be incredibly slow and sometimes imperceptible for some pupils. Teachers need to be helped to live with slow learning progress, to continue to feel responsible for the child's future learning without feeling implicated in their relative failure. In an educational system where educational success is defined in terms of comparison with some kind of norm in the rate of acquisition of academic learning, many children with special needs will have no place. Geoffrey Bookbinder (1984) writes, perceptively, about the expectations we hold for success in education.

> In any random population of children and in any area of learning, however, there will always be wide differences in the rate of progress. Such differences do not necessarily mean that there is something wrong with those at the lower end of the distribution. Yet the term 'learning difficulty' does normally have this connotation. It invites us to 'diagnose' the difficulty and provide 'remediation' for it.
>
> This confusion between normal differences in learning ability and a pathological condition within a particular child can be illustrated by using the analogy of height. Some children are significantly smaller than the majority of children of their age. Does this mean that they have growing difficulties?
>
> Let us take this analogy a step further. Suppose that the primary aim of schools was to produce good basketball players. Tall children with their ability to jump higher than small children would be the elite. The smallest children would find it difficult, if not impossible, to compete successfully and teachers might express concern about their jumping difficulties. The reason for their jumping difficulties, however, is not that they are small. They can, in fact, jump quite easily. It is because they are being asked to jump as high as others much taller than themselves. It is the nature of the unreasonable demands that causes the difficulties — not the fact that they are smaller than their peers. There is too wide a gap between what they are able to do and what they are required to do.

A support service which is hell-bent on helping teachers to achieve what for many pupils will be unobtainable goals, will produce predictable outcomes. Mainstream teachers will seek to avoid accountability for educational failure by identifying the *pupil* as the source of all problems. The result will be an increasing movement of pupils to some form of segregated provision. Special education becomes a system where the child's failure is legitimized by the formal processes of ascertainment. The teacher within the special school does not feel as implicated in an individual child's difficulties as the teacher in the mainstream school from whence the child came. Arrival in the special school validates the child as being the cause of the failure — not the teacher, not the curriculum, nor the teaching methods. Special school placement is a recognition that the child will fail and make limited learning progress. Indeed, historically the view has been that the 'successes' of a special school (those children who return to main-stream schools) represent a failure of proper initial diagnosis. Thus special schools can, at one level, be seen as operating within a 'failure model'. Within such a model the removal of any expectation of normality for the child can lead to lowered educational expectations and, sometimes, an unchallenging curriculum. What is required is not lowered expectations for children with special needs but a raising of achievable expectations both in terms of educational attainment and social behaviour. This implies a model which attempts to redefine what we mean by success for children with special needs. The exclu-sion of a sizeable number of children with special needs from ordinary schools prevents this job of redefinition from being carried out. An ordinary comprehensive school which had to define educational suc-cess for a group of seriously mentally handicapped children, might be better able, over time, to think about the meaning of 'success' for its remedial and slow learning pupils.

Support services have a significant part to play in enabling ordin-ary schools to engage in the process of redefining educational success. Coming to grips with the 'failure issue' will involve support services in processes which legitimize individual differences and variation between children in learning and social behaviour. An acceptance of individual differences is a necessary pre-condition for the development of optimal learning environments. This will involve an emphasis on appropriate and relevant long-term resourcing and adaptation to needs rather than expectations of 'curing', 'treatment' or the search for 'answers' to educational differences.

Towards a Rationale for Support Services for Children with Special Needs

While it is possible to identify optimal and 'progressive' future roles for psychologists, advisory teachers etc., it is considerably more dif-ficult to identify mechanisms for changing what they are doing now. A great deal has been learned about providing support to ordinary schools, yet a whole host of factors prevents radical reorganization, at LEA level, of the way in which support services operate. Some of these relate to entrenched views held by the 'supporters' themselves. Others have to do with the much greater problem of bringing about attitudinal and organizational changes in mainstream schools. These latter difficulties are in turn related to the resource implications which LEAs would face if they confronted squarely the issue of providing for children with special needs in mainstream schools.

Existing support services occupy the no-man's-land between two 'camps'. On one side are the schools — who, when attempting to provide for children with special needs, are often either inadequately resourced or poorly organized (or more often both). On the other side is the LEA — whose own resource limitations force them, at best, to throw a few more 'support' personnel into the fray, and cope with the individual casualties through the cumbersome statementing procedures. The current legislation leaves an ambigious situation with regard to responsibilities. The ball remains firmly in no-man's-land.

The present connection between support services and the issue of resources for children with special needs produces a confusing answer to two questions which need to be addressed by LEAs:

1 What role should support services play?
2 How many advisory and support personnel are required by an LEA?

There is a danger, at present, that support services are being developed by LEAs as an *alternative* to adequately resourcing ordinary schools to meet special educational needs. Only within a context where there exists a continuum of resources for special education needs can LEAs begin to define the need for and role of external support systems. Analysis of the 'resourcing issue' leads to a view that the immediate priority for LEAs should be to enhance and develop the ordinary school's own resources, rather than to further proliferate external support services. The aim should be to get provision 'closer to where the action is' — namely, within ordinary classrooms and within ordinary schools. This may entail making existing external staff progressively more school-based and should certainly be a guiding principle in the deployment of future resources. Policies of this kind will involve support services in some professionally uncomfortable tasks. For instance, it would mean that educational psychologists as a group actively resisted the idea that further increasing the size of psychological, advisory and other support services, operating externally to schools, will solve the 'problem' of special needs for their LEAs. The pressures to increase such services are enormous and do not come simply from psychologists themselves. As a response to the problem of making provision for children in ordinary schools it is cheap, expedient and, probably, in the long run totally ineffective.

Within the context of a resourcing policy for children with special needs in ordinary schools, it is possible to begin the process of defining what 'support' might mean. The needs of individual children, of ordinary schools and of the LEA as an organization will provide the framework of activities for support staff.

Individual Pupils

At present individual pupils provide the major focus for support services. Within an alternative rationale the numbers of children referred to or 'seen' by psychologists or advisory teachers would be small. These children who are seen by psychologists or advisory teachers will be those with severe, complex and lifelong difficulties. They will, in the main, be known to LEA support services well before the point of entry to formal education and few are therefore likely to be referred by ordinary schools. They will require additional, special and individual resource consideration, even within the context of an overall resource policy. Their problems will be relatively clear and determining their 'resourceworthiness' should not be controversial. This group will include the small numbers of children with serious visual/ auditory and communication problems where there is some discontinuity in terms of the teaching methods and expertise required. It will also include children with severe and multiple intellectual and emotional disabilities. Support services could profitably be involved with such children both at an indirect, advisory level and, alongside their teachers, at a direct interventionist level. For instance, advisory teachers for children with serious visual and auditory difficulties are likely to be involved in the planning of educational arrangements for such children throughout their educational career. In addition, the release of educational psychologists from irrelevant assessment and 'defining' work with large numbers of children should enable them to work cooperatively with teachers in designing individual, intervention programmes for pupils who test out to the limit the skills of all concerned with meeting their special needs. Educational psychologists, in this situation, would be working beyond the issue of defining resources and placements and becoming a resource themselves. If educational psychologists are to have a direct involvement with individual children (and it is hard to conceive of an educational or school psychology service in which they do not), then it must surely be with such children. Sustained, cooperative working between teachers, psychologists and other advisory/support staff, on the social, independence, communication and learning needs of our most handicapped children should offer exciting possibilities for all concerned. However, it is worth noting that the skills required of psychologists in this area, (if they existed upon entry to the profession), have largely atrophied over time. Considerable reorientation and retraining would be required within the profession.

Schools

Within the context of a resource policy for children with special needs in ordinary schools, the focus of support services would be to link with the resource and organizational structures developed by ordinary schools. Their job, in conjunction with these structures, would be to enhance and develop the ordinary school's response to special needs. Thus, rather than responding to the individual referrals of children from ordinary schools, support services would aid the ordinary school in developing its intervention strategies for all pupils regarded as having special needs. Having resources to meet special needs can sometimes create as many problems as having none. Ordinary schools will increasingly be faced with the challenge of deploying and organizing their resources effectively to meet needs. The organizational possibilities are not endless but there are a wide variety of possibilities depending upon the particular circumstances prevailing in any one school (see chapter 8). Just as external support services have traditionally been seen as providing the 'solution' to children with special needs, so schools can create identical expectations of their own special needs staff by the internal organization of provision, teacher rôles and responsibilities. Creating the elusive whole school approach to special needs is still largely an unmet challenge. Support staff, given their knowledge of, and exposure to, many different models of intervention and organization, can have much to offer ordinary schools, both in terms of advisory/consultancy work and school-based IN-SET. Models of organization and intervention represent one strand of input. A second major strand for any training approach would be to enhance the ordinary teacher's ability to *individualize teaching* for their pupils. INSET, would also need to develop the ordinary teachers *concepts of special needs*. Here, an emphasis on the relativistic nature of special needs and the need to make appropriate long-term adaptations to a wide range of individual differences amongst children will be crucial. An understanding of the concept of special educational needs will need to involve a clarification of 'special expertise' as no more than an extension of the ordinary teacher's skills. In addition, teachers should be enabled to reflect upon their understanding of terms such as 'educational failure' and 'educational success'. Rather than deskilling ordinary teachers, the emphasis of support work of this kind would be to re-affirm, reinforce and reassure teachers in ordinary schools, that they have the potential as teachers to meet the majority of the special needs which confront them.

LEA

Currently, LEAs employ educational psychologists, and to a lesser extent, other external support staff, to carry out the task of assessing and defining the resourceworthiness of individual children. The result of successful non-segregation policies would be to decrease the need for such work. Would LEAs still need to employ educational psychologists etc? This is the $64,000 question which lurks and provokes anxiety in the minds of many educational psychologists. The statutory requirement for educational psychologists to be involved in the 1981 Act assessment and statementing procedures provides a questionable rationale for multidisciplinary assessment (see chapter 4). Moreover, if LEAs limit the production of statements to children with severe, complex and life-long needs, the requirement for psychologists could decrease dramatically. However, the effective operation of policies of positive discrimination (chapters 2 and 3), expressed in terms of a continuity of resourcing (chapter 5), across ordinary schools will pose new demands and new needs upon LEAs. There will be a need, firstly, to develop a rational, objective and well understood system to underpin these developments. LEAs will need to develop a resource policy across the continuum of need. Secondly, authorities will need to monitor and evaluate the effectiveness of its policies. This will involve ensuring that resources earmarked and intended for groups of children whose special needs have historically been seen as having low priority, are effectively directed and employed at the school level to meet these needs. While this area of work could not be regarded as exclusively psychological in nature, a school psychology service would seem well suited to a monitoring and evaluative role of this kind.

The development of non-segregation policies could be regarded as threatening to the traditional roles of educational psychologists and a number of other special needs support personnel. However, it offers considerable potential for developing alternative roles and alternative areas of expertise. An LEA's educational psychology service is not necessarily exclusively concerned with special educational needs. The shackles of the educational psychologist's historical gate-keeping and defining role have largely relegated other potential contributions to an educational service to 'tinkering' activities. Within a redefined role, educational psychologists could begin to address the myriad of questions and problems that confront teachers and schools in and outside of special education. The largely un-met challenge for psychology and educational psychologists perhaps lies in the development of a psychology of schooling. Here a 'psychological perspective' — critical, analytic, systematic and evaluative — could contribute to issues of concern in the context of schooling. Currently, schools and the education service are having to address a range of concerns upon which psychology must impinge. Worthy of mention would be issues such as teacher stress, pupil profiling and assessment, teacher appraisal, and management and leadership in education. In addition there are continuing needs to develop optimum strategies, for example in the interviewing and selection of staff, in grouping policies in school, in pastoral care structures, in whole school policies etc. Educational psychologists are notably absent from any real involvement with these issues, which are central to schools and the education service.

Comment

This chapter has presented a critique of both support services to normal schools for children with special needs, and of the notion of 'special' expertise. What emerges is a view that ordinary schools do not primarily require an army of educational psychologists or advisory/peripatetic teachers to deliver their special expertise to growing numbers of individual children for whom the schools are inadequately resourced and/or organized. A rationale for the work of external support staff can only develop within a context of resourcing and management which enables the headteacher and staff of the ordinary school to make appropriate responses to children with special needs. Within this framework support services could increasingly work with ordinary teachers in a cooperative role, to develop skills, and to increase teacher sensitivities to a wider range of individual differences amongst pupils. These developments will not involve a simple transplant system, whereby special skills and special expertise are transmitted from the world of special education to mainstream teachers. The expertise required is possessed by both special and mainstream personnel. In-service training for special educational needs should, in LEAs, university departments and institutes of higher education, increasingly reflect the non-exclusive nature of special expertise. The development of a 'differentiated curriculum' to meet a variety of needs will involve support and training, coming as much from subject and curriculum specialists as from remedial and special personnel. Finally, and crucially, the point has been made that developing a curriculum which is sensitive to individual needs is intimately linked to a process in which 'success' in education is gradually redefined.

Chapter 7

From 'Non-segregation' to 'Integration' — Developing a Continuum of Provision

General Principles

Begin With the Ordinary School

Few educationalists would be prepared to publicly advocate and defend a policy of segregation for children with special educational needs. Some commentators have pointed out that the very word 'segregation', dominated by its initial sibilant 's', is perceived as something undesirable, in sound value alone. Post-Warnock and post-1981 Act, the idea of an LEA developing and making explicit a segregationalist policy would seem incongruous. Few aspiring special educational advisers are likely to gain a foothold within an LEA if they do not expound a strong integrationist line. Integration, it would seem, is the new orthodoxy in special education despite the fact that the majority of children with serious educational difficulties still receive a segregated education. Yet the picture is not as clear as it may seem at first sight. There remains within both special and mainstream education a strong belief in the value of segregated special education and a strong commitment to its maintenance. These beliefs are often held by individuals who, at one and the same time, show a commitment in both words and actions, to a more integrative approach. Thus, whatever the 'official' view is said to be, segregation and the need for special schools effectively acts as the *first principle* which guides policy in many authorities.

Segregational policies come increasingly into play as attention is focussed upon those children at the extreme end of the continuum of special needs. As we move away from considering the needs of the majority group of children with relatively moderate difficulties, and encompass those children with serious and severe handicaps, a some-

what different response seems to be called for. This applies particularly to two groups of 'special' children. In the case of children with
serious physical and/or mental handicaps and those children who
exhibit behavioural problems — the need for some form of segregated
provision appears, to many, to be inescapable. The apparent inevita-
bility of segregation for these groups is expressed in a number of ways
by LEA policy-makers. For example:

> There will always be some children for whom a special school
> is the only possible placement.
> There will always be a need for some special schools.

Such statements do no more than reiterate the received wisdom of
both the Warnock Report and the subsequent government White
Paper, *Special Needs in Education* (HMSO, 1980). The Warnock Committee expressed the view that '... We are entirely convinced that
special schools will continue to be needed ...'. A similar comment
was contained in the government White Paper '... In the government's view, it will continue to be necessary to provide places in
special schools and classes ... for some of the most seriously handicapped children'. The new orthodoxy of integration is limited, it
would seem, only to those who are 'integratable'. For the remainder
— an indeterminate number given the relativity of what constitutes a
special need — all routes lead to the special school.

The position adopted by a particular LEA on this issue has a
crucial bearing on the way in which special provision will be developed and organized. Frequently, policy-makers begin with the
view and assumption that 'there will always be a need for special
schools'. What follows is the development of procedures and the
deployment of resources to support this initial assumption. Discussion
focusses on questions such as: Which children should be placed in
special schools? How many special schools are required? How will
children be identified? What assessment and placement procedures are
required? How will schools be staffed and resourced? How will staff
be trained? etc, etc. Discussion of this kind swiftly removes the focus
from the whole issue of, 'making the ordinary school special'. Instead,
procedures and provisions are developed which confirm that special
schools are a necessity for certain children.

The suggestion here is that the first principle in developing a
continuum of provision for children with special needs is that we
'begin with the ordinary school'. The need for and place of segregated
facilities has to remain an open question. Whatever the current day-to-
day realities, it is important to hold in obeisance any decisions about

the ultimate need for segregated special education. Special s
not have a right to exist. They exist because of the lim
ordinary schools in providing for the full range of abilitie
abilities amongst children. It is not primarily a question of the quality
or adequacy of what is offered in a special school. Even a superbly
well-organized special school offering the highest quality curriculum
and educational input to its children, has no right to exist if that same
education can be provided in a mainstream school. Interestingly,
policy-makers in the field of special education, seem to fall into one of
two camps. The first group operates with an almost a priori assumption that segregated facilities will continue to exist. For the second
group the place of segregated facilities remains an open question; open
to be determined by the limitations of our policies in developing fully
comprehensive primary and secondary schools.

The principle, that we should 'begin with the ordinary school',
seems uncontroversial. Is it not a principle that all educationalists
would readily advocate? The suggestion here is that it is, indeed,
controversial. While a form of lip service will usually be paid to the
principle — commitment to the continuation of a segregated special
educational system is deeply ingrained, and, probably, widely held by
policy makers. Not surprising, perhaps when we consider that many
of the individuals currently concerned with special needs policies
have, themselves, strong historical and personal links with the segregated special education system.

The Principle of Non Segregation

The process of developing a continuum of provision for children with
special needs must begin by focussing attention on non-segregation
mechanisms. The majority group of children with special needs do
not require integration. The aim for this group, those with learning
and behavioural difficulties, must be the avoidance of segregation.
This can only be achieved by positive discrimination measures, resourcing policies, curriculum adaptations and support and training
initiatives which foster the ability of ordinary schools and ordinary
teachers to meet a diverse range of needs. The idea of integration
carries the connotation of children who are first separate, discrete and
different from other children. Integration is something to be offered
to a segregated group. Thinking in special education has been bedevil-
led by this approach. Questions are asked such as — 'How are we
going to provide for children with moderate learning difficulties, the

maladjusted or the language impaired?'. Categories or groupings of identified children who can then be offered either segregated or integrated education. Non-segregation implies a quite different set of questions that need to be answered. For example, how can ordinary schools meet the needs of all pupils in the community? How can we move towards the goal of providing access to a differentiated curriculum to meet the range of individual needs? Thus, in making provision for the majority group of children with special educational needs, priority has to be given to the development and elaboration of non-segregation policies rather than integration policies. Non-segregation policies will be closely linked to the goal of increasing, 'what is normally available' for children with special needs in ordinary schools. They will, if effective, combine to facilitate the development of whole school policies (see chapter 8) within all mainstream primary and secondary schools. Increasing what is 'normally available' will involve LEAs in policies and processes which are both complex and controversial. Pursuing the goal of non-segregation will involve all aspects of policy within an education service: from policies on pre-school education to policies on the design of school buildings; from policies on staff recruitment to the style and content of the school curriculum. Comments here will be restricted to a few important areas. One such area is that of nursery education.

Many children with special educational needs enter a segregated form of educational provision at a very early stage in their lives. Children with severe and multiple handicaps frequently enter special educational provision at 2 and 3 years of age. They become in the words of one writer, 'too special too soon' (Davis, 1984). Sometimes the unavailability of normal, nursery educational facilities, leads to a situation where pre-school provision in a special school is the only available option for a particular child. In other situations normal nursery provision does exist but children with special needs are excluded from it. 'Increasing what is normally available', needs to begin at the pre-school level. Pre-school children who have a range of special difficulties cannot be provided with non-segregated provision if no normal nursery facilities are available to them. *Thus the absence of universal nursery education represents a significant obstacle to the development of non-segregation policies.* The consequence, in many areas, is that professional workers, eager to enhance the development and socialization skills of young handicapped children and/or to relieve parents of total care responsibility, have little option but to gain admittance to segregated pre-school provision. In taking such a step the child's future educational placement is heavily prejudiced and, to some extent pre-determined. Arguably, pre-school children with special needs are, under the terms of the 1981 Act, the only group of pre-schoolers for whom the LEAs are duty bound to make provision. However, the Act is a double-edged sword. If adequate normal nursery provision exists, non-segregation policies can be implemented. Priority can be given to the admission of children with special needs in all of an LEA's nursery facilities, along with appropriate alterations in resourcing levels. However, in the absence of adequate amounts of ordinary nursery provision, all routes again lead to the special school.

Buildings and the physical environment of schools are also a major target for non-segregation policies. Schools, must be the only public buildings which can still be erected without due consideration being given to access, and to the toileting and hygiene needs, of the disabled. Few, if any, LEAs will 'make normally available' a right of access to ordinary schools for physically handicapped children. Lifts, ramps, corridor space and suitable toileting and hygiene arrangements for wheelchair-bound pupils are exceedingly expensive to install. Many such children have to be considered for 'integration' (perhaps into a special unit), or at worst, 'segregation' because of an inability to provide access to their local schools. The prohibitive costs involved in installing a lift in every secondary school, may, for the foreseeable future, mean that only a minority of wheelchair bound children will be able to attend their nearest ordinary secondary school. However, steps can be taken to improve what is 'normally available' in this respect. New schools are still being built in several areas of the country. An authority committed to non-segregation policies would ensure that within any future school building programme, questions of access, toilet and hygiene arrangements, as well as movement within and around the school campus, were *automatically* considered for the physically disabled. The majority of LEAs will need to consider modifications to existing premises rather than the design of new schools. If priority is given to earmarking finance on an annual basis, much can be done to enable 'minor works' such as the installation of ramps, the modification of toilets and changing areas and the purchasing of equipment to aid mobility, to be carried out. Situations frequently arise in LEAs where requests for relatively trivial sums of money required to carry out modifications of this kind, create untold administrative difficulties. In contrast several thousands of pounds for a residential special school can be found with relative ease. Establishing flexibility of funding within an LEA, in this area as in many others, can do much to aid non-segregation policies by increasing what can be made 'normally available'.

Resource policies which establish special educational needs as a priority/positive discrimination issue in all mainsteam schools (see chapter 5 for detailed discussion), represent perhaps the most potent of non-segregation measures. Resource policies, which operate at the level of schools or groupings of schools, rather than at the level of individual pupils, operate to define what should normally be available for pupils with special educational needs. Where broad positive discrimination policies, affecting all schools in an authority of this kind, cannot readily be implemented, alternative and more piecemeal approaches could be adopted. Selected ordinary schools can, as and when resources are available, have their provision for children with special educational needs enhanced. Schools may be selected on a variety of grounds, for example, a high internal level of social/special needs in a particular geographical location, or a primary school located in a rural area where alternative special provision is some miles distant. Schools may also be selected on the basis of their existing 'good practice'. Mainstream schools, particularly secondary schools, where children with special needs are treated positively and sympathetically often incur a form of 'punishment' as a result. As the school's reputation develops, increasing numbers of children with special needs are directed to that school at secondary transfer by staff in local primary schools, by educational psychologists and by a range of other agencies. This places the school's pastoral/remedial/special needs structures under increasing pressure. An LEA can, by moderate inputs of additional teaching, non-teaching and financial resources to such schools, support their work. Resource inputs of this kind would avoid placing pressure on the school to secure additional resources by statementing and the statutory mechanisms. Rewarding the 'good behaviour' of schools is as important an aspect in the field of special educational needs as it is in any other.

On whatever basis ordinary schools are selected for additional resourcing, certain guidelines can be usefully adopted. The rationale behind such policies is to increase the provision available in that school (or schools) for children with special educational needs, the aim being to avoid the need for future segregation of children. It should not be seen as a special unit. It would be important for schools themselves to decide upon the shape and use of whatever additional resources can be made available within a set of flexible LEA guidelines. The resources would need to be viewed as belonging primarily to the school and not to the LEA. A contractual arrangement between advisory and administrative staff of the LEA and the headteacher and staff of the school could operate. The headteacher and staff of the school might be invited by the LEA to develop a proposal for the use of certain specified staffing and financial resources. This proposal would then form the basis for discussion, amendment/confirmation with LEA administrative advisory and pyschological staff. Important amongst the priorities of the LEA would be the needs of the children with the greatest level of perceived difficulty and a concern to avoid any 'drift' of resources away from them, over time (see chapter 5). There should be no requirement for statementing of individuals as a result of the resource input. However in some schools, and within some LEAs, there may exist a need (administratively or politically) to 'record' certain children, or to specify numbers of children who are regarded as the prime recipients of the additional resources. Selective resourcing strategies of this kind can produce dramatic effects, both in terms of a reduction in segregation, and upon the requirement for support services to be involved in spurious individual 'assessment' practices (see chapter 6). They represent an anticipatory rather than reactive approach to special educational needs. Resources are provided to recognize existing needs and to avoid a future need for segregation.

Non-segregation policies need to operate within all aspects of the education service. John Fish (1985) comments

> ... because special educational needs are defined relative to the learning achievements of the majority, the organizations, curriculum and methods of ordinary schools, particularly as they impact on work with less successful learners, are major determinants of special educational needs. Thus any major policy for ordinary schools should now include consideration of its special education aspects.

Such policies would include areas in which new initiatives are occurring. Curriculum developments such as TVEI and CPVE represent opportunities for the involvement of pupils with special educational needs. They are initiatives which will change, in curricular terms, what is 'normally available' in schools. If children with special needs are excluded then the need for and familiarization with new technology and vocational training will become a further special educational need to be provided for other than in an ordinary school. Non-segregation policies need to operate, too, in the often more subtle areas of staff recruitment and career development for teachers. One interesting statistic, worthy of collection in any LEA, concerns the number of headteachers and deputy headteachers of mainstream secondary schools who, themselves, have had extensive, direct teaching experience in the area of remedial/special education. Double figures are unlikely to be reached by any LEA in England and Wales! Yet, the career development of teachers is a crucial area for special educational needs. If able and competent young teachers see little, or no, prospect of career advancement by working in the field of special educational needs, outside of working in special schools, the consequences are obvious. Consider instead the implications of an LEA policy where substantial and successful previous teaching experience of working with pupils with special educational needs, was an *expectation* of any candidate for a senior management position in a secondary school.

Keeping Provision 'Close to Where the Action Is'

The 'action', as far as children with special needs are concerned, occurs in schools and in classrooms. The activities which go on in education offices, advisory services, child guidance clinics and school psychological services are important, but can only be justified, insofar as they improve the quality of what happens between teachers and pupils in classrooms. We have, as yet, no evidence to suggest that the 'way ahead' in special education is to increase the ranks of external support services to the ordinary school (see chapter 6). There is an understandable temptation for LEAs to attempt to 'solve the problem' of children with special needs, and to 'solve the problem' of integration by increasing the level of services which operate outside of schools themselves. Thus, priority is given to increasing the ranks of educational psychologists, special advisory staff, coordinators of special needs and peripatetic specialists, etc. There are issues to do with both the economics of resourcing and the mythology of specialist expertise which underpin 'solutions' of this kind. There is a clear need for some advisory, psychological and other support services, which relate to the needs of children with educational difficulties. However, such services are not a substitute for adequate provision in schools and in classrooms. An adequate level of base resourcing in ordinary schools is a necessary requirement in order for support services to be effective. Priority in the allocation of available resources should go to staffing and resourcing, which has the greatest possible level of impact '... where the action is'.

Children's Needs Versus Professionals Needs

John Fish (1985) aptly describes this principle.

> Special educational arrangements should be developed on a service delivery model where the child needs them and not where the professionals prefer to work.

Needless to say this does not always occur. It would be comforting to feel that decisions about the educational placement of particular pupils were made on the basis of the child's needs. All too often, however, decisions are made to place pupils in particular situations because of the availability of speech therapy, physiotherapy or, at worst, the availability of transport. Paramedical services such as speech therapy and physiotherapy have grown accustomed to working with concentrations of their clients in special schools. The dispersal of children across a wide range of mainstream schools poses problems for their traditional service delivery methods. One parent of a mentally handicapped child commented — 'I have been offered Hobson's choice. Three sessions per week of speech therapy if I send him to the special school, one session per fortnight in his ordinary school'.

The development of non-segregation/integration policies poses considerable challenges to the customary practices of a whole range of educational and paramedical support services. The solution is usually seen to be the quest for more staff in order to do 'more of the same'. Thus, paramedical support services such as speech therapy will typically request increased staffing resources in order to 'deal with the implications of integration'. Instead what may be required is a radical reconsideration of what services such as these offer to children, schools and parents, and how the service is delivered. Thus speech therapy and physiotherapy may need to increasingly question the need for direct service delivery of their therapeutic skills to individual children. How much sense is there in operating a speech therapy service on an individual treatment basis to all pupils who have delayed speech and language development? Instead, a training/advisory role vis-a-vis teachers and parents may be a more profitable alternative for such services.

Principles of Integration

At some point non-segregation policies will break down. As we consider the needs of children with serious and multiple handicaps, as well as those whose behaviour has disastrous consequences for teachers and other pupils, we cannot realistically anticipate that non-segregation measures alone will meet either the needs of the children or the needs of the school. This is the point at which there is a move from non-segregation to integration and, perhaps, ultimately and unavoidably, to segregation. The need for the integration of a pupil might arise from a number of factors.

(i)   *Access to Schools / The Physical Environment:* The clearest example would be of a wheelchair bound pupil who is unable to attend the local mainstream school because of problems of access. The prohibitive cost, or practical impossibility, of carrying out necessary structural alterations may lead to a need to find alternative provision outside the child's neighbourhood school.

(ii) *Specialized Instruction / Teaching Methods:* There is nothing in this area which, theoretically, could not be provided for all pupils in their local ordinary schools. Practically, however, for a small minority, this is unlikely to be possible. Examples would include children with profound visual / hearing / language difficulties who require teaching by non-visual or non-oral methods. For such pupils there may be a need for a distinct and discontinuous form of teaching expertise linked to communication skills. Some centralization of resources / expertise in these areas is likely to be necessary. There may also be a social requirement for some of these pupils to be grouped together for some part of the school day.

(iii) *Distinct curricular needs:* This is a controversial and debatable area. All children have curricular needs which are in some way distinct from those of their peers. Indeed, a differentiated curriculum might be regarded as the hallmark of a school / classroom sensitive to individual needs. However, in the case of some pupils, particularly those with severe mental handicaps, the gap between their educational requirements and those of the majority of their 'normal', mixed ability, peer group will pose considerable practical problems for teachers and schools. The problem of meeting the needs of a 'one-off', mentally handicapped child in a mainstream primary classroom, is not solely to do with resources. While the needs of such a pupil may well be catered for in the early years of education, this will become progressively more difficult over time. The 'curriculum diet' required will become increasingly distinct and opportunities for group teaching and genuine social interaction and learning might become restricted. Curricular and social needs combine to make mainstream placements for this group of children difficult to sustain. Arguably, some form of 'integrated' provision, involving the grouping together of pupils with similar curricula needs, is required.

(iv) *Breakdown in Relationships/Tolerance:* This is perhaps the most controversial rationale for making alternative provision for children with special needs. Realistically, however, breakdowns in relationships do happen and will continue to happen. All schools, including special schools, have self-imposed limits in terms of the behavioural patterns which can be tolerated amongst their pupils. Non-segregation policies seek to broaden the acceptable range of normality of ordinary schools in this area. However, a tiny minority of pupils will exhibit behavioural patterns which are unacceptable in *any* school. Others, because of a breakdown in relationships in one school, will require an alternative educational provision. For the vast majority of such pupils, transfer to an alternative ordinary school, perhaps linked to a resource/support input, is preferable to placement in a special unit of some kind. There can be no educational or ethical rationale for justifying the grouping together of pupils, all of whom are displaying disruptive, anti-social, and frequently delinquent, behavioural patterns, in terms of those pupil's *own* needs. The plain truth is, that if the grouping together and segregation of children with behavioural difficulties is to be justified at all, it is on the grounds of benefit to other non-disruptive children.

(v) *Individualized/Small Group Teaching:* Children with a range of severe learning/developmental difficulties often require prolonged access to small group and individualized teaching. The limitations on teaching and staffing resources will usually lead an LEA to concentrate some, or all of its provision, for these minority groups of children with special needs. These are the children whom, it was argued (see chapter 5), have needs which cannot be readily predicted at the level of individual schools; children for whom the term 'disability' or 'handicap' might be appropriate. These are also the children who will need to be individually resourced.

There is, of course, much overlapping across these five groupings. For instance, children who have physical difficulties affecting
their access to school buildings, those who require specialized teaching
or a distinctive curriculum, or who have exceptional emotional needs,
will invariably require a greater degree of individualized and small-
group teaching. While all the factors listed can be regarded as contributing to a need for provision, 'beyond that which is made normally
available', none is a criterion for segregation. However, children at
the extreme of the continuum of special needs do pose a rather
different set of challenges to the mainstream educational system. A
variety of special arrangements and provision need to be made within
mainstream schools to meet these needs. These arrangements must be
compatible with meeting the, often unique, educational, developmen-
tal and personal needs of the most handicapped children in our communities whilst maximising the opportunities for integration with a
mainstream peer group.

Integrated Provision — Neighbourhood Schools

The American concept of providing the 'least restrictive environment,
for handicapped children' is a useful one when considering the development of a continuum of provision. It leads to a view that when
the need for 'special' provision arises, integration should occur,
whenever practically possible, in the child's local ordinary school.
Provision of this kind is, understandably, often the first choice of
parents of young children with special educational needs. It involves
their child attending, perhaps, the same school as other siblings,
friends and playmates in the local community. School is usually close
to home and the need for the potentially stigmatizing 'special bus/
taxi', is avoided.

Neighbourhood provision for individual handicapped pupils can
be extremely successful. Brennan (1982), in the context of discussing
physically handicapped children comments

> ... neighbourhood placements were outstandingly successful
> at primary level and showed considerable success in secondary
> schools also. Indeed the success, and the simplicity of the
> modifications required to meet special physical needs, raise a
> new question about the special schools. Are the elaborate pro-
> visions necessary for the individual needs of children? Or are
> they made necessary because 100 or so children with special

physical needs are brought together on one spot? Other associated questions also occur. How many children need regular physiotherapy as an essential part of their treatment? And how many receive it simply because it is there?

Neighbourhood provision usually relies heavily upon the use of welfare assistant (NTA) time, linked to individual pupils. Modification to buildings, toilets, etc., as well as the input of specialized pieces of equipment, are often also required. Physically handicapped and sensory impaired pupils are often the major targets of provision of this kind. However *many* other groups of special needs pupils could usefully benefit from this kind of provision including young mentally handicapped children and children with serious behavioural/ emotional difficulties. Neighbourhood provision is, however, not without difficulties. Welfare assistants and other non-teaching assistants are grossly underpaid and undertrained for the work they are responsible for in this, and many other situations within the field of special education. The value of the work of non-teaching assistants in special education is largely unrecognized, and merits close examination in terms of both research, and more importantly, in the provision of an adequate career and training structure. Arguably, their input needs to be supplemented by making available to ordinary schools some additional teacher time as well. This would provide staffing flexibility in order to enable the class teacher to carry out supplementary, supportive work with the individual child and/or to link with resources and services outside of the school, which are relevant to the child's needs. A particular problem of this kind of provision is the possibility of a child with exceptional difficulties being isolated from special resources and teaching techniques appropriate to his/her needs. Thus some organized links between the neighbourhood school and relevant specialist, advisory/paramedical services is usually essential. It is in this area that advisory teachers, for example, for hearing and visual impaired children, have a particularly important role to play. Similarly, a young mentally handicapped child integrated into the local primary school could profitably be linked with an existing resource base (a mainstream or special school facility) which had experience in and knowledge of meeting needs in this field.

Special Provision — Selected Mainstream Schools

For any of the variety of reasons previously discussed, neighbourhood provision may not, in the long term be a practical possibility. Integration must then occur within a mainstream school beyond the child's immediate neighbourhood.

Most LEA provision for children with serious educational difficulties exists within separate special school settings. If integrated provision is developed it is usually done using the 'special unit model' — the creation of a miniature special school within the mainstream. Units are usually developed along single handicap lines, using a discrete physical base within a normal school. Units can provide a useful alternative to a segregated special school placement but can also be fraught with difficulties. While no blue-print exists for the development of integrated provision of this kind, both experience and research evidence (for example, Hegarty, Pocklington and Lucas 1981; Cope and Anderson, 1977) would indicate that attention could usefully be focussed upon the following areas.

Location

Provision of this kind is something consciously added by an LEA to a mainstream school to provide for children with serious educational difficulties. The children will usually be drawn from a relatively large catchment area. Such provision is distinct from resource measures taken by an authority to improve what is 'normally available' within any one school for the school's own children. For this purpose, schools need to be selected which can offer a highly favourable environment for a group of highly vulnerable children. The attitudes of headteacher and teaching staff towards children with special needs is probably the most important criterion for the development of successful provision. Personal attitudes are sometimes difficult to assess. Perhaps the best indicator in this area would be the school's commitment to, and success in, providing for children with more moderate difficulties *presently* within the school. A school which is providing well for its slow learning and disadvantaged children, a school which has a high tolerance for its behaviourally difficult pupils is likely also to succeed with a group of more seriously handicapped children. The quality and calibre of *existing staff*, particularly any involved primarily with children with special educational needs, is also an important factor in the selection of an appropriate school. The additional staffing and resources to be provided by the LEA will need to be integrated with any existing remedial/special structures. Few things can be more damaging to the integration of a specialist facility than its fragmentation from other special and remedial structures within an ordinary school.

A third factor concerns the existing level of special needs within any proposed mainstream base. It would seem sensible to place any additional special provision within a school which has a balanced intake of pupils. School which are heavily overloaded by children from socially disadvantaged backgrounds may not form the ideal location. Their major concern must be to meet their own, internal, 'special' needs. Similarly, schools which have a very low level of internal needs may not be able to maximize the advantages of accommodating a 'special' range of children. Much of the benefit of provision of this kind comes from extending special resources to some children within the mainstream school who have more moderate special needs.

Geographical location and the availability of accommodation, physical space and particular amenities for toileting and hygiene purposes, are important (but not, perhaps, the most important) aspects. A resource base, central and integral to the school, is likely to be necessary, but the aim would be for the children concerned to be linked, for many curricular activities, to a mainstream class, thus minimizing the need for separate rooms and facilities.

Children

Historically special units within mainstream schools have developed as a response to the needs of a specific group or category of handicapped children. Thus, we are familiar with units for the 'hearing impaired', units for 'language impaired' children, units for 'the ESN(m)' etc. There are a number of problems with this approach if the aim is to both maximize the opportunities for integration of handicapped children and to encourage non-segregation measures for other children with special needs. Firstly, 'unitization' by handicap grouping relies heavily upon the development of criteria for defining who should be included (and excluded) from the proposed handicap group. For instance, who is to count as being 'language impaired' as opposed to the new euphemism — 'moderate learning difficulty'? 'autistic' as opposed to 'mentally handicapped'? 'mentally handicapped' as opposed to 'physically handicapped'?, etc. Provision of this kind can also produce a curious attempt on the part of professional workers to 'seek out and find' children, to fit the category group. Thus, it can easily become a system to encourage segregation. Secondly, provisions which are developed for discrete categories of handicap usually operate to prevent other children with special needs from benefiting from the special resources provided. One of the great myths that has developed in the field of special education is that there are clear differences between the curriculum and teaching needs of the various handicap groups. Currently, we have a system which encourages the *search for differences* rather than the search for similarities between children with special needs. What is required is a model for the development of provision which looks for similarities, both between children with special needs and their non-special peers, and between the various handicap groupings within the field of special education. What is being proposed is essentially the 'integration of the categories' (see Dessent, 1983). Thus, we should look towards the development of special needs facilities and resources rather than discrete units catering for 'learning difficulties', 'behavioural difficulties' and so on. How far can we go along this path? What about the 'hard' handicaps: visual impairment, hearing impairment and physical handicap? These latter groups both more easily attract resources and are more readily accepted by mainstream teachers and thereby present fewer problems for integration into schools. Traditionally, units for children with sensory and physical handicaps have been isolated from other areas of special need, whether within special or mainstream schools. But the reality is, that many children with sensory and physical handicaps have multiple difficulties and their curricula needs are not widely dissimilar from those of other groups of children with special needs. There will, of course, be a need for specialist teaching and equipment for some groups, particularly those requiring teaching by non-oral or non-visual methods. Certain designated mainstream schools may need to be staffed, resourced and physically equipped to provide for these minority groups. However, what is being suggested is, that even these facilities should be open to any pupils, with significant special needs, who can benefit from the small teaching groups and general climate of these specialist resources.

There are many advantages to the development of 'generic' as opposed to specific facilities of this kind. Not least it confers some of the advantages (financial, attitudinal, 'acceptance') of high status special needs groups (for example, sensorily and physically handicapped children) upon the low status — 'maladjusted' and 'learning difficulty' groups. It is difficult to imagine how a resource base for 'children with special needs' in a primary school, could maintain a physically handicapped child with complex learning and perceptual difficulties and a visually impaired child with associated learning difficulties on an integrated programme, but be unable to cater for a physically normal, socially deprived child with learning problems. In developing generic facilities in mainstream schools specialist provisions should be extended to encompass children with more moderate difficulties within the base school. What needs to be avoided is the operation of a dual special needs system — special and remedial operating cheek-by-jowl within the same school.

Organization

Special facilities which are consciously developed by LEAs within mainstream schools could usefully be organized around two key principles. The first is concerned with *maximizing the opportunities for integration*. This will involve attention being paid to both the integration of staff as well as the integration of children. The 'problem' of integrating special needs staff can only be totally avoided by having none! There are always likely to be problems of 'grafting on' teachers, usually from another teaching background, with experiences and expectations which differ markedly from those of their mainstream colleagues. Insufficient attention is being given by LEAs to staffing strategies which do not rely upon this 'limpet' model of developing provision (Jones, 1983). An alternative approach would be to base special provision upon a 'whole school' approach. Here a designated school could develop its own 'whole school' model to deploy whatever additional resources are made available by the local authority. This might involve organizational strategies quite different from the unit and unit teacher model. For example, if its resources are flexible a school might decide to make alterations in the composition and size of all classes throughout the school; to make maximum use of non-teaching staff; to develop flexible small group and withdrawal methods for all class teachers or to develop the expertise of particular members of the schools *current* staffing. Where a decision is made to employ specific specialist teachers, the integration of the 'special' staff is made immeasurably more difficult where an LEA pays the divisive 's' salary allowances to special educational teachers working in mainstream facilities but not to their colleagues responsible for 'ordinary' classes. Payment of 's' salary allowances should be avoided and if necessary replaced by a suitable placement on the normal Burnham scales.

As well as a range of child and curriculum skills, specialist teachers need to possess some essential skills in consultation and negotiation. Above all, they need credibility with mainstream staff. Such credibility is, perhaps, best engendered by successful mainstream teaching experience. Ensuring that 'special' teachers participate fully in all school activities, and that they have a significant and regular mainstream teaching commitment, can also be helpful in this respect. For instance, within a secondary school, specialist teachers could be closely identified with particular subject departments and seen as being members of these departments.

The successful integration of teaching staff is, probably, a necessary precursor to the successful integration of children who have significant educational difficulties. Ideally, all such pupils would register in, and be regarded for pastoral purposes as part of, a mainstream class. Withdrawal from mainstream activities would be on the basis of the minimum which is compatible with meeting their specific needs. What needs to be avoided is some arbitrary statistical notion concerning the 'ideal' level of integration which a child should or could have. Levels of integration depend totally upon decisions which are made by mainstream and special teachers concerning the deployment of their available resources and the accessibility of particular curriculum activities. The most severely handicapped child can, in both theory and practice, be integrated for 100 per cent of their day.

A second important principle for the development of integrated provision is that special facilities should be resourced and operated so as to convey *no disadvantage to the base school*. Stated more positively, developments of this kind should convey clear advantages to the whole school. The resourcing implications of integrated facilities are rarely fully recognized by either LEA officers or ordinary schools themselves. Staffing and financial resources must be *at least as good* as those made available to pupils with similar special needs who have previously been placed in separate special schools. Enhanced resourcing cannot be restricted only to teachers and ancillary staff who have special needs responsibilities. The location of a special needs facility in an ordinary school will need to involve reconsideration of the school's overall staffing and financial resourcing, in order to ensure that the children concerned can enjoy a range of experiences linked to normal classes. Ideally, class sizes throughout the school should be kept as small as possible. Establishing a low maximum number for *all* classes might be an appropriate step to take. There would probably need to be increases in staff at all levels: teachers, ancillaries, as well as secretarial and, perhaps, dinner supervisory staff. Children with high levels of physical, medical, personal and educational needs will place heavy demands on the school's personnel and material resources. Facilities of this kind will also increase the management responsibilities of headteachers and senior staff of ordinary schools. The managerial functions formerly carried out by the headteacher of a special school are not lost within integrated provision. Thus, LEAs will need to recognize the increased managerial role of senior staff in mainstream schools via their resourcing strategies.

Provision Outside of Normal Schools — The 'Ownership' Principle

The issue of the 'ownership' of special educational resources has been a recurring theme in previous chapters. The ownership of special resources is intimately linked to the ownership of responsibility for teaching and educating children with special needs. The suggestion here is that, wherever and whenever special educational provision is made, the ownership of that provision should be progressively devolved to mainstream schools themselves. Successful integration of children with special needs seems to occur when ordinary schools feel that they, rather than the LEA or anyone else, own both the resources and the responsibility for meeting the special needs of their children. Fostering ownership by mainstream schools within the framework set by agreed LEA guidelines, could be seen as a desirable aim for *all* forms of special educational provision. The ownership principle should certainly relate to any off-site special units. The proliferation of off-site units for disruptive pupils has occurred largely without the involvement or managerial responsibility of mainstream headteachers and teaching staff. Off-site provision of this kind, like special schools, is seen to 'belong' to agencies and individuals outside of the ordinary school. The removal of a disruptive pupil to a special unit rarely implies any loss of teaching or financial resources for a mainstream school. The suggestion here is that, wherever a need is perceived for educational facilities for children with special needs outside of ordinary schools, the management of such facilities should fall to the headteacher (or headteachers) of the mainstream schools served by the provision. Sayer (1985) extends the ownership principle even further.

> Any off-site special units should be part of the management of ordinary schools, whether or not they remain physically separate. Those additional services not at present defined as 'special' but related to special services should be similarly brought into the mainstream community management of schools: educational social workers, multi-cultural appointments, careers service, child guidance services. So, eventually, should social services.

What of special schools themselves? The movement to link special schools with mainstream schools, either via 'a twinning principle' (Booth, 1983) or via a resource link (Dessent, 1984) are, perhaps, the initial stages of bringing separate special schools within the management and resource structures of mainstream education. The proposals of the Fish Committee (1985) to devolve responsibility for meeting special educational needs and to cluster mainstream schools together with special educational facilities and services, is a further embryonic example of 'the transfer of ownership' and responsibility to the mainstream. Given the economic realities of the 1980s devolution policies which lead to a more local approach to educational services are likely to become commonplace. 'Clusters' within the ILEA, 'Local Financial Management' in Cambridgeshire (Hinds, 1982), and sector-based provision in Oxfordshire (Jones, N. 1983) are likely to move the ownership of special education increasingly into the hands of local mainstream headteachers. These broadly-based organizational changes in the way in which the whole education service is managed and resourced may, over time, have more impact on the integration/segregation issue than any number of government reports and Acts of Parliament.

Comment

The focus in this chapter has been on the development of a continuum of provision for children with special needs within mainstream schools. A series of principles which might underpin such a continuum have been described. Table 6 provides a summary of the continuum in terms of four levels of provision and resourcing. Such a continuum would stretch across the age range from pre-school education to further education in schools and colleges. In this model, the majority group of children with special needs — those with moderate learning difficulties and a range of social behavioural problems, including those currently placed in special schools and units — would be catered for at level 1. A variety of non-segregation measures operate at this level which increase, 'what is normally available for children with special needs in ordinary schools'. Thus the local mainstream school becomes the starting point and the finishing point for most children regarded in some way as being special. Beyond level 1, the focus changes to that of integration. Here, the concern is for children with severe, complex and usually long term difficulties, who clearly require individual consideration and resourcing to meet needs. Integration will ideally occur at level 2 within the local neighbourhood school.

Table 6: A continuum of mainstream provision for children with special educational needs

Level 1   Non-Segregational Measures — Increasing 'What is Normally Available'

— Resource policies
— Policy on school buildings
— Policy on pre-school provision
— Curriculum, training and career development policies.

Level 2   Special Provision — Neighbourhood School

— Enhanced teaching and non-teaching provision
— Specialized equipment
— Use of advisory and other specialist resources

Level 3   Special Provision — Selected Mainstream Schools

— 'Generic' special needs provision
— Special resources integrated within selected mainstream school environments.

Level 4   Special Provision — 'Off-Site'

— Facilities which operate as part of the management and resourcing structures of mainstream schools.

In some cases, particularly when dealing with multiple handicaps or sensory difficulties requiring alternative communication methods, provision may need to be made within selected/designated mainstream schools (level 3) and, exceptionally, within 'off-site' facilities (level 4). In the latter case it is suggested that a direct management/ 'resource ownership' link is established with mainstream schools. The numbers of pupils requiring integration is ultimately determined by the adequacy of the non-segregation measures taken by a local authority. The successful operation of non-segregation measures will have the effect of facilitating an effective response from all mainstream schools to their own pupils with special educational needs. It is this area, the development of whole school approaches to special educational need, to which we now turn.

Chapter 8

Whole School Approaches to Special Educational Needs

'All teachers are teachers of children with special educational needs'.

The Case For a Whole School Approach

Highland Junior School is involved in some important changes. The school's response to these changes illustrates the importance of a whole school approach to meeting special educational needs. Two major developments are occurring. Firstly, the social mix of the school's catchment area has, over a period of years, altered dramatically. Professional, skilled and semi-skilled families, attracted by new housing developments in smart, suburban areas, have progressively moved away from the inner city environment served by Highland. The school now provides for a preponderance of children from relatively disadvantaged home backgrounds. Unemployment is rife and free school meals the norm. The skills of children, both on entry to the school and on leaving at age 11 are dramatically below the level of any national norms. Historically, the school has provided for its 'special needs' pupils by means of a full-time remedial class, taught by an experienced and capable teacher. Children with the most serious learning difficulties were drawn predominantly from the first three years of the junior age range and taught, almost exclusively, within the secure base of the remedial classroom. 'Remedial' children, whose difficulties appeared intractable or who demonstrated a range of additional social needs, were frequently 'referred' to outside agencies with a view to placement in a local special school. This is the second area in which changes seem to be occurring. The headteacher had, over the past two years, noticed a marked reluctance on the part of both parents and the LEA support services to consider special school place-ment. Consequently, the staff at Highland felt that they were now having to cope with children who in previous years would have been regarded as special school candidates.

In the past, the school's method of dealing with children with special needs had seemed to operate well. The head saw the remedial class as an economic use of a scarce resource — a capable and experi-enced teacher who demonstrated considerable personal interest in the needs of slow learning pupils. The removal of some of their 'most difficult to teach' pupils was usually welcomed by other teaching staff and seen as enabling them to devote more of their time and attention to the 'average' and 'more able'. Shortcomings were, of course, re-cognized. There were never enough places in the remedial class for all potential candidates. Pressure came each year for the class to become bigger (at one stage numbers reached twenty-three). The children concerned did not experience as wide a curriculum as their 'non-remedial' peers because of the need to provide concentrated coach-ing and practice in basic skills. In addition, remedial children were thought to experience some name calling and teasing in the play-ground. Not all parents were happy for their son/daughter to go into the remedial class. However, for some time, the perceived advantages of this pattern of provision were seen to outweigh any disadvantages. Now, both headteacher and classroom teachers felt that the school was under tremendous pressure. They appealed to the local authority for some additional resources to cope with the increased demands of its altered client group. A rapid piece of screening indicated that approx-imately 40 per cent of the children in the school were thought by teaching staff to have some kind of special need. The need was seen to be for more remedial help; perhaps a second remedial class, or at least some form of withdrawal from mainstream lessons. After all, ordin-ary class teachers were not, the headteacher argued, trained and equip-ped to cope with 'these' children. Off the record he was prepared to admit that a few members of staff could not respond adequately or sympathetically to slow learning and behaviourally difficult pupils — neither had they any knowledge of remedial materials and resources. The school's remedial teacher was coming under increasing pressure from class teachers to take out of ordinary classes children who were, in their words, 'just not coping with the normal curriculum'. The children seemed to be in need of continuous small-group attention.

The problems confronting the school were well known to the LEA. Resources were tight, but eventually some extra teaching time was found and added to the school's remedial provision. This extra resource was greeted with enthusiasm (and relief) by staff at the school. An additional remedial withdrawal system was formed with a further forty or so pupils receiving short bursts of remedial attention, in small groups, outside of normal classrooms. Yet, despite the extra help available to the school, the provision still appeared inadequate. There remained a sizeable number of pupils untouched by the school's special provision. Those receiving help appeared to make only marginal gains, despite the extra individual attention, and, on their return to ordinary classes, continued to struggle ... the 'special needs problem' at Highland School remained.

Highland school lacked a 'whole school' response to special educational needs. Whole school approaches represent the new 'Holy Grail' within the field of special education — much talked about, advocated by all but difficult to find in practice. The concept of the whole school approach offers an exciting alternative to traditional forms of organizing special, or remedial, provision within ordinary schools. As John Fish (1985) comments, 'To put it crudely, many schools in the past made remedial and other arrangements with two needs in view. Learning difficulties would either be cured or children with them would be taken out of circulation to avoid disrupting ordinary children ... Problems arise because many schools either plan provision on the curing assumption or on the segregation assumption'. The 'curing' and 'segregation' philosophies are closely related to a 'within child' model of special educational needs. They still dominate the way in which most secondary and primary schools organize whatever resources they have available for children with special needs. Hinson (1985) notes, 'Most secondary schools in England and Wales continue to operate either special classes or withdrawal groups, or a combination of both. Remedial education tends to be concentrated on the 11–14 age range with little provision for 14–16 year olds, although many schools regard the work of lower sets in English and Mathematics as fulfilling this role'. Similarly, within mainstream primary schools the important survey conducted by Croll and Moses (1985) produced a picture of special help being provided, predominantly for basic literacy skills, on a withdrawal basis usually by part-time teachers without any special training or qualifications.

These traditional practices have increasingly come under attack. The concern for the integration of pupils previously placed in special schools has had a knock-on effect within the ordinary schools themselves. Special classes within ordinary schools, and indeed, systems of extensive withdrawal from mainstream classes, are being questioned, both from an ideological point of view and on the basis of research findings. In the case of the latter, schools are being confronted by an almost total absence of research evidence demonstrating the effectiveness of special class provisions on children's academic attainments, in comparison with placement in mainstream classes (for example, Galloway, 1985). In addition, it is questionable that there are any long-term benefits of withdrawal for remedial teaching. This is particularly true where such support is unrelated to the mainstream curriculum, where it ceases upon the child's return to ordinary classes and where little or no attention is paid to what is subsequently on offer in that classroom (Galloway and Goodwin, 1979; Galloway 1985). One of the interesting findings of the study by Croll and Moses was that, in spite of the enthusiasm amongst primary teachers for withdrawal, *the majority of teachers did not believe that the pupils' learning difficulties would be overcome.*

The value of special educational provision made outside of the normal curriculum and the normal class is thus being questioned. This is happening in a context in which school ethos, school organisation and the nature of the curriculum are being seen as crucial in defining and engendering special educational needs. As Wildlake (1985a) comments, 'It is obvious that attempts to treat learning difficulties cannot be confined to more and more intensive work with individuals, however desirable it is to increase our understanding of, and empathy with, particular pupils'. As interactionist concepts of special needs gain ground, the solution, rather than increasing the level of separate special provisions, is seen in terms of affecting changes in the nature and organization of 'whole schools'. The curriculum is seem as both the main cause and potential cure of many learning difficulties. All teachers are seen as having the prime responsibility for dealing with learning difficulties — the class teacher in the primary school and the subject teacher in the secondary school. Meeting special needs becomes the cross-curricular exercise par excellence.

Establishing a Whole School Approach

It is in this area, the development of whole school approaches, that we can glimpse the potential which special education has to improve, and indeed revolutionize, our schools and our system of education. An 'ordinary' school aiming to develop a whole school approach will quickly perceive not only the enormity of the task and the obstacles to be confronted, but also the wide ranging implications for educational practice for all teachers and all children. The whole school response will essentially be a response to meeting the *individual needs* of children. As such it is not just about the size and shape of a school's special needs department — although the work of such a department will be vital. It is not just about meeting the needs of handicapped children or an ill-defined group who are 'below average' or who are slow to learn. *It is about all children regardless of age, family background, race and aptitude.* A whole school approach will impinge upon all aspects of schooling. It will involve tackling some fundamental questions. Questions of value in education will be paramount. What is education for? Whose purposes does it serve? Which children does the curriculum exclude and include, and why? It will address issues concerning the way in which schools are organized and in particular the way in which pupils are grouped for teaching purposes. It will affect teaching methods. It will need to address fundamental issues such as the relationship between parents, the community and the school. Finally, and perhaps most importantly, it will affect school curriculum, by which is meant all the opportunities for learning provided by a school. The search for a whole school approach to meeting special needs runs parallel to the search for a 'differentiated curriculum' — a curriculum responsive to individual needs.

Establishing a whole school response to children with special needs will pose an enormous challenge for mainstream schools. Few are likely to have moved beyond more than the initial stages of evolving the structures, ethos and shared attitudes and approaches which are necessary. Realistically, in most schools, a lengthy time scale will be needed in order to bring about change. There are, however, some practical, initial steps which can be taken by schools. Some of which will be outlined in this chapter.

Questions of Value and Attitude

Whole school approaches to meeting special needs begin and end with questions of value, philosophy and the attitude of teachers and headteachers. The pursuit of a differentiated curriculum will always be limited within a school context which does not recognize, reward and value diversity amongst children. Even where an individual school is committed to finding ways of valuing all of its pupils equally, a curriculum responsive to individual needs could not be guaranteed. Without such values it is probably a non-starter. One of the characteristics of successful special schools lies in their capacity to value children for what they are, and to continue to value them regardless of their sometimes destructive and self-destructive behaviour. David Galloway (1985) links the hidden curriculum of school values and ethos to the occurrence of disaffection and disruption in schools.

Pupils with special needs frequently have a low self-concept. This can be related to a feeling that their efforts and achievements are not valued. It can also be related to a feeling that they are not acquiring new skills, relevant to their immediate interests and future needs. If these pupils see academically more able pupils deriving personal satisfaction from school activities, receiving approval from teachers and parents, they will necessarily find ways to protect themselves from their sense of failure.

School ethos and values, along with the attitudes of teaching staff, make up the 'hidden curriculum' of a school. Revealing what is hidden is rarely an easy matter. However, we can be clear about some of the attitudes, values and practices which might be conducive to the development of a whole school approach to meeting special educational needs. *Child centred* as opposed to predominantly subject/ discipline centred teaching seems to be one (but only one) of the hallmarks of teachers who are successful in showing children that they are valued as individuals. This is not a denial of the value of teachers who are authoritative and knowledgeable within a particular discipline. Rather, it indicates that for such teachers to be successful as *teachers* requires important additional interpersonal skills and that priority is given to the needs of the child as an individual learner. The essence of a child-centred approach must be that of respect for children as individuals and a concern for their rights and welfare.

Secondly, the valuing of individual children regardless of background, abilities and disabilities would seem at odds with an educational climate geared essentially *to competition and comparison between individuals*. Within such a climate, children with special needs will always be losers. Success, progress and achievements are relative to the individual and the reward system of the school would need to reflect this. Primary schools geared principally to the needs of an able minority, or secondary schools dominated by the needs of the external examination system, are unlikely to be able to develop curricula and forms of organization which place an equal value on all children. The Hargreaves Report, *Improving Secondary Schools* (ILEA, 1984) included comments from a number of individuals concerned with the problems experienced by children in the secondary sector. A Divisional Educational Welfare Officer commented as follows:

... the comprehensive secondary school appears to be largely based on the needs of the smaller proportion of the more able, mature and home-supported pupils, whose educational needs are primarily cognitive and exam-orientated, rather than on the needs of the larger proportion of less able, often less mature and sometimes less home-supported pupils whose needs are not just cognitive and are often not exam orientated, but are also emotional and social. As one of my colleagues says, 'At present it is all geared to the public examination system: the central focus is not the child'. The many less able academic pupils therefore seem to be educated in the slip-stream of the smaller proportion of academic ones, rather than their needs being the central focus of the curriculum planning and organization of the schools.

The extent to which certain skills, curriculum areas and aspects of knowledge are differentially valued within schools is also important in this respect. The Hargreaves Report has drawn attention to the historical tendency for schools to accord greater value to academic and theoretical activities as opposed to practical skills and applied knowledge. Many schools will frown upon 'able' pupils who opt to develop practical and technical skills at the expense of accruing qualifications in 'academically respectable' areas of the curriculum. For children who struggle to achieve competence in the basic skills of literacy and numeracy, the implications of such a value system are clear. That which is practical, that which is social, that which is 'recreational' and that which is sometimes seen as extra-curricular needs to be increasingly regarded as educationally respectable. The skills involved need to be valued by teachers and parents as much as they are by the pupils themselves.

If the values, philosophy and aims of a school are of paramount importance in developing a whole school response, then the role of the head teacher is, as usual, central. No school is likely to develop fully such a policy — affecting as it does all aspects of schooling — without the full support and backing of the head. The head's role is vital in facilitating and leading curricular and organizational changes. It is equally essential in ensuring positive discrimination in the use of available resources, and in pursuing a staff recruitment policy which progressively enables a whole school approach to be shared by all members of the school staff.

Pupil Grouping and School Organization

The way in which a school groups its pupils represents one of the most potent indicators of its value system and the hidden curriculum. Galloway (1985) comments,

> Selection by ability cannot easily avoid creating a hierarchy within the school, in which higher status is ascribed to pupils *and* their teachers at the top of the hierarchy and lower status to those at the foot.... Teachers in low ability or special needs classes may emphasize the intrinsic nature of the task through an emphasis on mastery learning. They may even achieve a high level of success. Their success, however, will be in spite of, and not because of, the school's policy on academic organization. The reason is that the teacher's emphasis on the intrinsic value of the work the pupils are doing is inconsistent with the dominant philosophy in the school which is likely to equate ability with status.

Mixed ability teaching is really only a live issue in secondary schools. The vast majority of primary schools in Great Britain, freed from the shackles of selection at the age of 11, have had mixed ability classes for a number of years. Individual and small group learning approaches have been developed as a response to meeting diverse pupil needs. Thus, grouping policies are intimately related to the perceived goals of schooling (for example, exam credentials in the secondary school) and to teaching methods (whole classes versus individual/small group learning).

Meeting the full range of special educational needs in the ordinary classroom represents the ultimate step in the process of extending mixed ability teaching. It is clearly a form of organization which is hugely more demanding of teachers than systems of streaming and setting which create more homogenous groups. Thus, the value of mixed ability teaching needs to be considered in the context of overall values and aims. It also needs to be considered within the context of what constitutes a viable group size for *any* effective learning to occur and within the context of other grouping criteria such as age (see Sayer, 1985). If we take as our starting point the idea of a class of thirty and one teacher, if we assume that we are dealing with pupils of similar age across the whole ability range including one or more with serious individual disabilities, if we match this with a curriculum and teaching methods geared to knowledge acquisition and the pursuit of examination credentials — then we have a non-starter. It seems unlikely that any pupil's individual needs can be met in this context, let alone those of a child who has exceptional needs. Successful mixed ability teaching can only be achieved within a resourcing and curriculum framework which makes it possible. Such a framework is likely to involve a range of small group and individual learning experiences, flexible teaching methods and extensive supportive inputs to the teacher.

Methods of grouping pupils represent only one aspect of school organization. Effecting a whole school response to special needs will involve attention being paid to a number of organizational aspects. The way in which schools set about issues such as parental involvement, pastoral care, discipline, the planning of the curriculum, timetabling and the organization of teaching will greatly influence their ability to respond to individual needs.

Within a whole school approach, two principles are likely to be central in deciding upon organizational structures. *The first concerns the importance of the ordinary classroom teacher.* Kathleen Luton (1986) commenting on her experiences as a teacher working to coordinate special needs provision in a large secondary school, comments as follows, 'The ordinary classroom teacher is the most important and undervalued resource that a school has, and the practice of integration requires them to be even more flexible and inventive, not always with sufficient additional resource.'

The increasing specialization of roles and functions of those working inside schools as well as those supporting 'from the outside', has often led to a deskilling of the ordinary teacher. In the area of special educational needs the class teacher's job in the primary school and the form tutor's role in the secondary school has often come to be that of 'referring' the child on to someone else — remedial teacher, year head, psychologist etc. The organization of pastoral care responsibilities in both primary and secondary schools can operate in a similar way. Personal responsibility can be removed from class and form teachers and taken on by headteachers, year heads and other senior staff. Whole school responses would, instead, establish the class/form tutor as having the prime responsibility for each child's personal, social and educational development, and would then work to provide the necessary resources and support for them to be effective in this role.

A second principle concerns the *importance of cooperative planning and teaching* in meeting special educational needs. One teacher within four walls and behind closed doors, working out his or her own salvation with a class of children, still represents the dominant image of teaching in this country. If it remains that way, whole school responses are unlikely to get off the ground. Kathleen Luton comments, 'Unless there is a strong element of shared responsibility and shared problem solving, together with a desire to facilitate learning for all abilities, a school will never be able to make much of a whole school policy for students with special educational needs.' The very notion of a whole school policy implies teachers working together to arrive at shared understandings and meanings about what constitutes a special need, what constitutes a relevant curriculum response to such a need, and how a whole school can respond. Christine Gilbert's (1986) description of developments in a London borough secondary school illustrates this aspect of cooperative planning and decision making.

> Between January and July 1983, various staff working parties met, and in September, a formal consultative structure was set up which encouraged staff collaboration in the review and development of all aspects of the school's work. To encourage joint planning, it was agreed that the school should close early one day each week so that teachers could meet in departmental, and less frequently, year teams. After school on other days, cross-curricular committees of interested staff were also set up to examine aspects of the school's curriculum and organization. Well over half the staff participated in these groups. The structure facilitated the establishment of active and supportive teamwork.

If cooperative working is important in establishing a whole school framework, it is an essential aspect of actually meeting special needs. This may involve cooperative working between teachers; cooperative working between teaching and non-teaching staff and cooperative working between teachers and parents. While the ordinary class/ form teacher is the focal point for meeting special needs in the ordinary schools, adequately supporting their work will involve a range of cooperative enterprises with other personnel. Christine Gilbert (1986) describes a range of such activities at her school, including cooperative teaching between members of the school's learning support team and subject specialists, as well as in-class support for children with special needs across a number of curriculum areas.

Organizing Support for Special Needs

The way in which an ordinary school organizes and deploys its 'special' resources will have a crucial bearing on whether or not a whole school policy is developed. There is a curious paradox here. The existence of a separate structure — 'a special needs coordinator'; 'a special needs department'; 'a compensatory education department' or 'a learning support department' — could be seen as hindering the development of a whole-school response. Often, this is exactly what happens in practice. Those teachers who carry responsibility for special needs can develop working practices which, sometimes inadvertently and sometimes more consciously, have the effect of stripping other teachers and other departments of responsibility for meeting special educational needs. Maintaining the 'mystique of the expert' is one aspect of the way this can happen (see chapter 6). In a Utopian world, the full realization of a whole school policy might negate the need for a separate organizational structure for meeting special educational needs. In the same way the realization of 'whole authority' approaches could obviate the need for separate, special administrative and advisory staff (see chapter 3). For the present it seems certain that ordinary schools will require a focal point for developing initiatives and new responses to diverse, individual needs. The question is, how should such support for special needs operate?

What things are called is of some importance. There are almost as many names and labels for teachers concerned with special educational needs as there are schools which employ them. 'Remedial' has given way to 'special' — particularly with the implementation of recent legislation. Thus 'special needs coordinator' and 'special needs department' are some of the contemporary labels in this field. While such terms represent an improvement, in that they recognize a broader definition of educational difficulty than simply those of learning problems, they suffer in other respects. 'Special' implies some kind of categorical grouping of children, a special department may be seen as implying the place where teaching for such a group should occur, or where 'special' expertise exists. Better perhaps, is an emphasis in name on the role and function of personnel as supporters of learning — thus 'learning / curriculum support teacher' and 'learning / curriculum support department'.

Status is of importance too. Not least to the career development and salaries of the teachers concerned. Within a large primary school, scale posts, assigned to teachers with responsibilities in the area of special needs, are becoming increasingly common. This is an important step forward *so long as their responsibilities relate to developing and facilitating whole school approaches.* Within the secondary school, teachers responsible for developing the school's response to special needs ought to be members of the school's senior management team. If special needs is to be a whole school, cross-curricular enterprise, then it must affect all aspects of decision making within the school. Thus, the teacher carrying major responsibility in this area would need to be on a par, at least, with heads of subject departments. Further, specific responsibility for special needs would need to be one of the accountabilities of a deputy head within a secondary school. How this would operate would depend upon the particular structure and organization within any one school. One method might be to include the task of coordinating and developing special need's provision within the responsibilities of a deputy head (pastoral).

Within both primary and secondary schools it is necessary to consider two particular organizational aspects, if the aim is to develop a whole school approach. Firstly, there should be a concern to avoid *fragmentation* of responsibilities for different aspects of special educational need. For example, some primary schools may house a special unit or a special facility of some kind for a particular group of children. When this is the case there is the possibility of two separate 'special structures' operating within one school. 'Special' and 'remedial' splits of this kind have, in the past, been commonplace. The new nomenclature introduced by legislation can even involve a dichotomy between 'special' and 'special — special'. Within a large secondary school, fragmentation of this kind can be rife. Christine Gilbert (1986) pinpointed the following facets of special provision which existed within her London borough comprehensive school:

Head of Remedial Education
Teacher in Charge — Special Unit for Disruptive Pupils
Teacher in Charge of Delicate Unit
Part-time Teacher (English as a second language)

Where such fragmentation occurs, the possibilities for duplication of work and effort, and conflicting aims and philosophies are considerable. Coordination of teaching staff whose training, experience and role expectations may differ considerably can lead to controversy. It implies a form of teamwork, cooperative working and a shared commitment to a style of working. Specific and specialized skills are seen as a resource to all, but are de-emphasized in terms of organization. Instead, generic teaching skills are emphasized, as are the needs which 'categories' of children have in common.

If the first step is to ensure coordination of a school's special resources, the second must be to ensure that 'ownership' of that resource is invested in the ordinary structures of the school. Thus, ordinary class teachers in the primary school, subject department staff and form tutors in the secondary school, need to 'own' the school's special resources. Organizationally, ownership can be conferred in a number of ways. Equally, and too easily, it can be retained within a separate special structure by the particular organizational framework adopted by a school and the role played by support staff. For instance, a *total* reliance upon special withdrawal groups in both primary schools and secondary schools is unlikely to move the ownership of responsibility for children with special needs away from the staff doing the withdrawing, towards those responsible for teaching the pupils back in the ordinary class. A large and discreet special need's department in a secondary school, operating independently of the school's pastoral system and subject departments would be inappropriate for similar reasons. Lip service is often paid to liaison between classroom/subject teachers and staff who withdraw children for specific purposes. In reality, the problem of liaison is rarely solved unless it is built into the fabric of the school's organization. Some helpful developments in the organization of support systems within ordinary schools have emerged in recent years which bear upon this issue.

Primary Schools

The traditional organization of primary education, with one teacher assuming major responsibility for all aspects of children's learning and social well-being, provides a useful framework within which individual special needs can be met. The recent emergence in some LEAs of 'designated' teachers, and scale-post holders in the area of special needs, can provide an important focus for the development of whole school policies. Such teachers are likely to be full-time, able to pursue training and INSET opportunities and to establish links with external support services. Developments such as this represent a significant departure from the 'part-time remedial lady' image of remedial education. The questions concerning roles and responsibilities still remain. Other responsibility posts, for example in curriculum areas such as language and environmental studies, do not carry the implication that post holders will be directly responsible for teaching language and environmental studies to all children in a primary school. Yet, too often, this is the assumption behind remedial and special posts. Thus the teachers concerned may be described as 'acting as consultants' for other staff but, in practice, spend most of their time teaching withdrawal groups. 'Ownership' continues to reside with the designated teacher. An alternative form of organization might involve a scale-post holder in having responsibility for a mixed ability group in the same way as other members of staff, albeit with a less than full-time commitment. Any additional teaching resource which the school may have (for example, part-time staff, teaching input from the headteacher) could then be used to 'free' the designated teacher and, where the resource permits, other classroom teachers from classroom responsibilities for a proportion of time. This could enable the scale-post holder to engage in a variety of activities to support and develop the school's special needs policy. It may include any of the following: cooperative 'support' teaching with another member of staff; developing a resource bank of materials for the school; liaison time with other teachers and external agencies; coordination of additional resources (for example, non-teaching assistants and parents); withdrawal work with particular individual children. If class teachers could also be freed, even for a limited period of time, this would permit them the opportunity to assess, establish firm relationships and develop individual programmes for children in their own classes. The problem of liaison is greatly reduced when it is the class teacher who devises the individual programme (drawing upon the advice and resources made available), and then implements it within his or her own normal classroom environment. While patterns of organization of this kind are beginning to evolve in primary schools, other aspects conducive to a whole school approach are more firmly established. Important to note is the increasing use made of parents and non-teaching assistants as a valuable resource in meeting special educational needs. There is now a burgeoning literature on the use of parents, mainly in the area of children's reading development (for example, Tizard, Schofield and Hewison, 1982; Bushell, Miller and Robson, 1982; Topping and Wolfendale, 1985). The evidence which is mounting in this area, usually concerning primary-aged pupils, offers a significant challenge to traditional forms of organizing support for children in ordinary schools. Should, for instance, a school allocate a proportion of a teacher's time to coordinate a parent reading scheme for its less able pupils, rather than to spend the time withdrawing pupils for additional assistance outside of ordinary classes?

The work of non-teaching assistants (NTAs) is, in contrast, poorly researched. However it is an area of work which is of increasing importance in both primary and secondary schools. The NFER study of pupils with special educational needs in the ordinary school commented as follows:

> Teachers identified ancilliary staff as a major resource in educating pupils with special needs. Apart from attending to care needs, which was often the initial reason for employing them, they could provide a level of support that freed teachers to concentrate on teaching and reduce demands of a non-teaching nature on teacher time. In some schools ancilliary staff were given a more specifically educational role, either working with one or more pupils under the teacher's instructions or implementing a programme drawn up by a visiting speech or physiotherapist. (Hodgson, Clunies-Ross and Hegarty, 1984)

For many years NTAs have played a vital *educational* role within special schools. Their work has been largely unrecognized by LEAs and is poorly rewarded in terms of salary. Now, NTAs feature significantly as a resource in supporting children with special needs in ordinary schools. The numbers of such staff are increasing in many authorities. Their work with individual children, in this context, can sometimes be seen as controversial. This is particularly true if NTAs are (mistakenly) seen as a cheap alternative to the provision of extra teachers, or where teaching staff are unaccustomed to cooperative forms of working in the classroom.

Secondary Schools

In recent years provision for children with special needs in secondary schools has come under close scrutiny. Much rethinking has occurred concerning the role of teachers with remedial/special responsibilities. This questioning and rethinking is part and parcel of the current 'crisis in secondary education' where every facet of the organization, curriculum and aims of secondary education has been called into question. While traditional patterns of special needs provision (special classes, bottom sets and extensive reliance upon withdrawal) still predominate, the rapid changes which are occurring are reflected in a spate of recent journal articles (Lewis, 1984; Edwards, 1985; Hockley, 1985; Wildlake, 1985b). Most of these developments have in common, either the aim of facilitating the response of curriculum subject departments to special needs, or of moving special provision into mainstream classes. Thus, ownership of responsibility for pupils with learning difficulties, together with the ownership of the school's special resources, is seen to reside increasingly with subject areas rather than within a separate special enclave. The 'resources approach' to meeting special needs in the secondary school is one example of a model of working with these aims in mind (Jones, E. 1983; Jones and Berrick, 1985). As described in practice in Oxfordshire, the 'resources approach' involves special need's staff in a variety of supportive work with mainstream colleagues — preparing materials, acting as 'consultants', monitoring and assisting individual pupils within mainstream classes — as well as more traditional work with groups and individuals withdrawn from the normal class. More radical and wide-ranging developments in support work are occurring, as part of a new national policy initiative in Scotland. These developments, described by Blythman (1985) and Booth (1985), followed from a document produced by the Scottish HMI (SED, 1978). Booth summarizes the main recommendations of the Report as follows:

> The Scottish report placed the major responsibility for the creation of learning difficulties on the narrow focus and method of presentation of the curriculum in schools. It gave remedial education a broad definition, arguing that up to 50 per cent of the school population could experience learning difficulties. It suggested that, rather than provide a casualty service for school failures, remedial specialists should have a direct, and officially sanctioned role in supporting class and subject teachers to develop differentiated curricula through planning, consultation and cooperative teaching.

The Report stressed that, 'appropriate rather than remedial, education is required'. The intention was that mixed ability learning and teaching would be extended and that the withdrawal of pupils would be kept to a minimum. Central to the report was the specification of a new role for the specialist remedial teacher. This was to be a multi-purpose role encompassing four main strands:

(i)   acting as a consultant to staff and members of the school management team;

(ii)   providing personal tuition and support for pupils with learning difficulties in the early processes of language and computation;

(iii)   in cooperation with class and subject teachers providing tutorial and supportive help in their normal classes to pupils

with learning difficulties in the later stages of these processes;
(iv) providing, arranging for, or contributing to special services within the school for pupils with temporary learning difficulties. (Blythman, 1985)

The development of new roles for special needs teachers, and new forms of organizing special provision within secondary schools, usually entails consideration of two interlinked issues. The first concerns the role of subject departments in meeting special educational needs. The second concerns the use and nature of 'support teaching' between special needs and subject area staff. Whole school approaches to special needs must, by definition, concern themselves with the way in which each subject area plans to respond to the full ability range. A number of possible organizational options exist. Where there is a sizeable special needs department, a decision could be made to allocate each member of that department to a subject area. The aim being to assist, for example the maths department, to identify core concepts to be taught in their subject, and to develop their curricula, resources and materials to meet a wide range of needs in ordinary classes. The member of staff concerned would be involved in attending departmental planning meetings, and a variety of working patterns might evolve, including cooperative team teaching. A potential problem to be overcome in this situation concerns the responsibilities and accountabilities of the support teacher — is he/she responsible to the head of support services or to the head of the subject department? Who ultimately 'owns' the resource?

An alternative organizational strategy would be for each subject department to nominate a member of staff to be responsible for developing that department's own response to children with special needs and to provide a link person for the school's support staff. Important questions here might be concerned with the status and standing of designated staff within their own department. Other alternatives exist. For instance it may be argued that 'inserting' *one* support teacher into a subject department or, indeed, nominating *one* teacher within a department could serve to undermine the responsibilities which every teacher has to respond to diverse pupil needs. One response to this kind of difficulty would be for a school's support staff to work cooperatively with *all* teachers within one department, intensively, for a specified block of time. Within this period the aim would be to support individual pupils, to sensitize staff to the needs of pupils, and to develop flexible teaching approaches, curricula and learning materials. Thereafter, intensive working links could be developed with other departments, with an in-built maintenance system for pupils/ departments previously given support (see Gilbert, 1986).

Whatever form these departmental links may take, it seems likely that *support teaching* will need to feature as part of a whole school approach. Support teaching is an important part of the new initiatives occurring in Scotland, and is receiving increasing attention in secondary schools south of the border. The term 'support teaching' encompasses a wide spectrum of activities and roles. Its meaning will vary from school to school depending upon the extent to which the support teacher's work affects what happens in ordinary classrooms. At one level the support teacher is seen almost, as Tony Booth notes, as a technologist, '. . . offering the means by which existing curricula can be adapted to the level of the learner, or to the disability of pupils'. At the other end of the spectrum, genuine cooperative team teaching occurs where support staff are, '. . . intimately concerned with understanding, challenging and devising curriculum content'. In between, and probably most representative of the support teaching which is currently occurring in our secondary schools, secondary staff work within mainstream classrooms to support identified pupils with special needs as an alternative to withdrawal (see Edwards, 1985, for a sensitive account of this kind of work).

Whole School Approaches — Some Issues Arising

Whole school approaches to special needs open up at least as many new problems and questions as they attempt to resolve and answer. One problem relates to the issue of economy of effort, time and resource. Whole school approaches imply a breaking down of specialist domains and responsibilities and a movement towards *generic practices*. Mixed ability groupings and cooperative teaching require careful planning, preparation and monitoring. Time is required to plan, liaise, cooperate and evaluate. Where will the time come from? Some may come from the release and spreading of the resources of special needs support staff, which has been previously confined to withdrawal situations. It seems unlikely, however, that this on its own will be enough. Schools attempting a support teaching role may rapidly conclude that it is impractical to provide support to all curriculum areas, all age groups, and to all the individual pupils seen to require support. Support teaching may come to be seen as less cost effective than traditional practices. The result will be a return to withdrawal as the prime method of support. Booth and Pym (1982) comment '. . . One of the reasons for a division of labour between ordinary and special education may be the limited time in which teachers are expected to fulfil an unlimited job description. Whether their role as managers of special services can actually be accomplished within their daily schedule depends on whether the degree of support they receive actually frees them to accomplish this task.'

The problem here is, firstly, to do with having an adequate level of resourcing, and secondly, of being certain about aims and objectives. Support teaching, as part of a whole school strategy, is not just an alternative to a remedial, withdrawal system for a specified number of pupils. The aim is different. It aims to affect the quality of curricular experience in ordinary classrooms for all pupils with unmet needs. This may imply some losses in terms of intensive individual input to certain pupils. This particular dilemma is clear in Ferguson and Adams' (1982) critical appraisal of team teaching, using remedial specialists, in the Grampian region of Scotland. The authors conclude

> ... It is difficult to see how remedial teachers can operate within a classroom and yet provide the individual treatment, personal interest and concentrated attention which, it . was earlier argued, is of particular benefit to remedial pupils. Helping the subject specialist to ask better questions, provide more attractive materials or get round the whole class so that everyone's written work is seen before the end of the lesson, is a useful contribution which makes for better teaching. But it is still necessary to question whether improving the quality of teaching for all children is the most effective way of providing extra help for children with learning difficulties.

Support teaching has overlapping, but nevertheless different aims and objectives to traditional remedial withdrawal. In this area, as in many others, more integrated methods involve a 'trading off' of advantages and disadvantages as set against more segregated forms of organization. Is exposure to a broad subject curriculum more or less important than intensive small group practice in basic skills? Are the social advantages of interaction with a full ability range of peers more, or less, important than building up the pupil's self esteem within a protected special grouping? Are social aims more important for an individual pupil than gains in academic skills? Answers to questions such as these will ultimately reflect individual values although they can be informed by educational research. In reality, most schools will probably hedge their bets, settle for a 'mixed economy' of provision and operate both support and withdrawal systems. Withdrawal methods are not necessarily inconsistent with a whole school approach. They offer advantages for some pupils in terms of their individual, small group context and the opportunity for relationship building which they offer. To be effective they require collaboration between support teachers and mainstream staff — communication, liaison and joint planning. In effect they probably require as much teacher time for planning, liaison and inter-staff communication as do team teaching approaches. To see them as a more cost-effective alternative to support teaching probably indicates a misunderstanding of what withdrawal as a teaching method should consist of.

A second major issue raised by whole school approaches concerns the skills, presumed expertise and training required, in order that special needs staff are able to adopt these new roles. The traditional skills of screening, diagnostic assessment and intensive remedial treatment in basic skills, all practiced in glorious isolation from the mainstream curriculum, seem peculiarly out of place within a support role. Are support teachers now to be seen as experts in learning? If so, does this imply that subject teachers are not? It seems unlikely, as Ferguson and Adams (1982) note, that it is possible to act as an expert in learning difficulties without making reference to the content of the curriculum. 'Difficulties do not occur in a vacuum, and it is not entirely convincing to claim to be an expert in learning and at the same time to admit that one is not to be trusted to teach maths, science, technical subjects and so forth, to pupils who find these subjects difficult'.

If support teachers cannot claim exclusive expertise in processes of learning, perhaps their raison d'être lies in the area of consultancy. Skills in consultancy and cooperative working feature significantly in the document prepared by the National Advisory Committee in Scotland, for a new advanced diploma course in learning difficulties. The Committee listed the following 'general skills' as being appropriate for teachers working to support children with learning difficulties in primary and secondary schools.

— Expertise in the processes of consultancy.
— Expertise in working with individual pupils with learning difficulty.
— Ability to cooperate with colleagues and others.
— Ability to formulate and maintain a broad view of the curriculum.
— Skill in providing, contributing to or arranging for special services for pupils with temporary learning difficulties. (extracted from Blythman, 1985)

Thus, equal stress is laid upon the skills required in working with other adults as is placed upon working directly with individual pupils. Skills of cooperative working and consultancy are writ large. Yet similar questions can be asked here. To be successful, team teaching between a science specialist and a secondary support teacher, and cooperative working between a primary class teacher and a learning support teacher, require skills of cooperation and liaison from *all* parties involved. Thus a training course with these objectives offers no answer to those in search of a unique form of expertise for special educators. Perhaps the movement towards support teaching roles, rather than representing a new and exclusive role for special needs staff, should be seen as part of a more radical development of cooperative working between *all* teachers as a response to meeting diverse needs in a mixed ability classroom.

Comment — In Search of a Differentiated Curriculum

The development of a differentiated curriculum — a curriculum adapted to the abilities, backgrounds and interests of all pupils — is the ultimate goal of a whole school approach. Such a curriculum will not arise outside of an educational philosophy which nurtures and facilitates it. The first questions to be addressed are questions of value rather than of educational technology or, indeed, questions concerning the organization of special needs provision. However, prevailing values, attitudes and educational philosophy will not always be conductive to these ends. When this is the case the seeds of future change in a school's value system will sometimes need to be sown by incremental and individual shifts towards different forms of organization and cooperative working.

Chapter 9

Parents, Homes and
Special Educational Needs

Parents as a Force for Change in Special Education

Parents are a potent force for change in the field of special education. To some extent this has always been so. Historically, parent pressure groups have been important in obtaining special provision for disability groups such as the hearing impaired and the mentally handicapped. Their latent power and ability to effect change in the nature and the location of special provisions has now been reinforced by the 1981 Act. Moreover, we are probably only at the beginning of a process of increasing parent power. Recent legislation in education has done little more than reflect wide ranging changes in our society concerning the power of the consumer in determining the pattern of public services. The idea of 'parental involvement' and 'parents as partners' can no longer be regarded as controversial in education. In the field of special educational needs, pre-school home intervention programmes such as Portage have encouraged many parents of handicapped children to exert greater control over the educational decisions made about their children. Some LEA administrators are now well able to recognize a Portage Parent!

Parents of children with special needs usually express a preference for 'mainstream integrated' provision (Hegarty, Pocklington and Lucas, 1981; ILEA, 1985). Sometimes this preference is expressed in an organized fashion, for example, The Parents Campaign for Integrated Education in ILEA. Moreover, the work of the Advisory Centre for Education, the Children's Legal Centre and the Spastics Society (Centre for the Study of Integration) can provide additional support to parents seeking mainstream provision for their children. *There is every reason to believe that parents who are insistent, persistent and unswerving in their requests for integrated (or indeed segregated) resources and provision will be successful.* The ability of parents to influence decision-making in this area makes the efforts of teachers, educational psychologists and a range of professionals look ineffectual by comparison. LEAs may be able to afford to ignore the advice of those they employ to advise them. They cannot quite so easily ignore the 'advice' of the parents of children they are paid to serve. To a large extent, policy in special education in Great Britain, at the present time, is being formed around parental choice and parental pressure rather than any overriding educational or ethical principles.

However, the relationship between parents and the special education system is by no means straightforward. Certainly parental pressure does exist. Sometimes it is exerted by individuals and sometimes by groups of parents. But how representative are the views of these individuals and groups of the wishes of all parents? Usually it is an informed and articulate minority of parents who place pressure on LEAs for more integrated provision for children with special needs. Often the views of parents of children with 'recognized' handicaps, for example, Down's Syndrome or the Hearing Impaired, are the only ones that are heard at both local and national level. Voluntary organizations exist as a focal point for most forms of mental, sensory and physical handicap. In contrast, we need to ask which parent group is representing the views of parents of children with learning and behavioural difficulties? Where is, for instance, the parent-led National Association for Children with Moderate Learning Difficulties? It was the parents of children with these kinds of difficulties which the Fish Committee in the ILEA singled out as requiring additional help and support. The Committee made the following observations about children with emotional and behavioural difficulties.

> We found it indicative of the problems which these special needs create that we had difficulty in meeting groups of parents, and those parents whom we did meet tended to have children who had other significant problems or handicaps. No voluntary or parent's organization appears to represent their interests.

There is a very real danger that parents of children with special needs will increasingly fall into two groups — an articulate minority, hell-bent on 'mainstreaming' and a silent, ill-informed majority who, in the absence of a voiced opinion, will be offered 'segregation'. Thus, one could envisage a situation where large numbers of children with evident handicaps are integrated into ordinary schools, whereas the vast majority of children with special needs, those with moderate learning difficulties and/or social difficulties, remain in segregated provision.

This is but one possible scenario. Alternatively an increasing number of parents of seriously handicapped and disabled children may opt for placements within special provision which has historically been utilized for children with more moderate problems. These parents may view such provision as the 'least restricted environment' in the absence of adequate integrated provision in ordinary schools. Thus, special schools and units for children with moderate learning difficulties may increasingly provide for a more handicapped clientele. These schools would then encompass the more able of those pupils previously located in schools for the seriously mentally handicapped, alongside a group of children with complex difficulties which they have not traditionally accommodated. There will then be a knock-on effect throughout the special educational system. Those schools previously catering for a broad range of mentally handicapped children will encompass only those with multiple disabilities and associated, severe behavioural problems. Within this scenario, pupils with more moderate educational difficulties should increasingly find themselves within mainstream schools. To some extent these two possible scenarios, both resulting from parental pressures, are reflected in changing patterns of special provision within many LEAs at the present time.

An increasingly insistent, and politically important voice, is coming from another parental group — the dyslexia lobby. The dyslexia issue is one of those educational cans of worms which rates alongside issues such as streaming and mixed ability teaching in terms of its ability to generate heated, and usually fruitless, discussion. This group of parents is politically important in the field of special educational needs because of its *potential* for representing the interests of *all children with learning difficulties*. While the dyslexia lobby hangs on to its exclusive, specific and pseudomedical underpinnings, this potential will not be realized. It will remain at the level of a pressure group for primarily anxious, middle-class parents. The outcomes for most will be expensive, private and often dubious 'assessments' followed by equally expensive and questionable private tuition. The odd foray will be made into the LEA 'statementing' bureaucracy — most of which will be contained and redirected. Instead, what is required is a parent-led organization which will embrace the needs and rights of all pupils with learning difficulties. This would include children who have, historically, been provided for in special schools, special units and remedial departments. Such a pressure group could do more to engender changes in LEA resource allocation policies than any number of statements for dyslexic pupils.

Parents are a force for change. Ultimately, however, their concerns are (quite rightly) for their own individual child. Their aim must be to secure what they see as the best possible teaching environment and resources for their child. Harnessing these individual pressures for change to enhance facilities and provisions for all pupils is a task for teachers, schools and the LEA. Developing *generic* provisions (see chapter 7) is one way of achieving this. Thus, parental pressures for resources for particular groups of children (for example, specific learning difficulties, hearing impaired, physically handicapped, autistic,) can be reflected in provision which can be extended to other groups of pupils where the parental voice is rarely heard.

The Special Needs of Parents

The past twenty years have seen something akin to a revolution in the way in which parents are viewed in relation to the educational process. This revolution has been reflected in terms of government reports and legislation, parental involvement projects and developments in the fields of special education (see Wolfendale, 1983 and 1985). In many respects, special education has led the way in this area. Work with parents of children with special needs has been well documented. Notable examples include the work of the Hester Adrian Research Centre (Mittler and McConachie, 1983); the Child Development Research Unit at Nottingham University (Newson and Hipgrave, 1982) and Portage Home Visiting Services (Cameron, 1982; Dessent, 1984b; Daly *et al*, 1985). Work in this area increasingly stresses the positive contribution which parents can make to their child's education and development, their skills as teachers and their rights to be involved in, and contribute, to decision making. As Sheila Wolfendale (1985) notes:

> It is clear that parents are being acknowledged as *contributors* to children's development and education. Nowadays they are regarded far less as clients with the client characteristics of being dependent on experts' opinions, passive in the receipt of services, apparently in need of redirection, peripheral to decision-making and perceived as 'inadequate', and 'deficient'.

This 'new' perspective on parents is a healthy one. Nevertheless, it is only one side of the coin. The parents of children with special needs are not always able to make a positive response to their child's needs. Nor can they always be regarded as a positive teaching resource to be harnessed and directed by helping professionals. Parents have special needs too. If ordinary schools are to become special they will need to be able to respond, not only to the special needs of children, but also to the special needs of parents. In the extreme, they will need to be able to respond to the special needs which are sometimes engendered by a child's care and home background.

The importance of special education as a response to family and parent needs cannot be overstressed. Many children 'arrive' in a special educational setting *primarily* because of family, domestic and parenting difficulties rather than because of the strictly educational difficulties of the individual child. For some children this occurs because of the 'punishing' effects that the demands made by parents have on ordinary schools and ordinary teachers. The social definition and causation of special educational needs is clear in this context. Many families have multiple needs and can be demanding of time and attention from staff in ordinary schools. The social and family difficulties which parents frequently discuss with class teachers and headteachers will often alarm and frighten the teaching staff concerned. This may precipitate a move towards referral and the sharing of responsibility for the problems with outside agencies.

The link between social disadvantage, family and domestic difficulties and the incidence of special educational needs in children is very apparent in the case of children with learning difficulties and those with social and behavioural problems. A report prepared for the ILEA on the characteristics of pupils in different kinds of special schools and units summarized its findings in this area as follows:

> The relationship between social factors and different kinds of disability was reflected by the social composition of different types of special schools. Pupils at schools for emotional and behavioural difficulties and, (to a lesser extent), those at schools for moderate learning difficulties and for delicate pupils, were particularly socially disadvantaged. A higher percentage of pupils at these schools were eligible for free meals, more had parents who were unemployed or had semi- or unskilled manual jobs, and a higher proportion came from single parent families. (ILEA, 1984b)

The child who arrives on the doorstep of the local special school arrives with not only an individual educational problem. He/she is also more likely to have experienced many of the stresses caused by urban living, poverty, unemployment, inadequate housing or family discord.

Disabilities which have a physical or medical origin do not show the same relationship to social background factors. Nevertheless, they produce, and are related to, a whole range of additional needs. Parents of seriously physically and mentally handicapped children face immense practical problems in coping with the needs of their child. They face considerable emotional stresses concerning the present and future care of the child and the handicap usually impinges on all facets of family life. Not surprisingly, the problems confronted by such families are often, over time, seen to require responses over and above that of special educational provision for the handicapped child. Residential special schooling often has its roots in the need to relieve parents of some of the day-to-day burdens of caring for a handicapped child. Thus, whether a child's special needs are seen to result from disadvantageous home circumstances, or where handicap engenders additional family needs — special education is often seen as a solution to the problems raised.

Special Education as a Response to Parent and Family Needs

One of the clearest, but least publicised characteristics of successful special schools lies in their commitment to responding to the social, personal and community needs of their pupils and their pupils' families. Special schools have no monopoly on this kind of response. Nevertheless, it is an area of work which has probably seen a great deal of development within the special school sector. Mike Marra (1984) has described a variety of strategies employed in a special school for children with moderate learning difficulties, to facilitate supportive links with parents. Significantly he states, 'As a head teacher of a special school, I feel an obligation actively to encourage staff to involve themselves with parents in home visiting as one of the professional responsibilities of teaching children with special needs'. Many mainstream schools will be involved in this kind of activity with certain pupils as a matter of course. However, in many ordinary schools, particularly secondary schools, it is not seen as part and parcel of the job of teaching. For many teachers it involves a fundamental change in the nature of their role and their relationship with pupils and their families. It requires a blurring of distinctions between meeting educational and social needs. Some teachers will regard it as 'social work' rather than teaching. Yet it seems unlikely that special educational needs can be effectively met unless teachers in ordinary schools increasingly adopt some of the best practices of existing special schools. 'Integrated' children will lose out if teaching staff do not extend their responsibilities beyond the confines of the classroom into a concern for the whole child within the context of family and community.

The ultimate extension of special education into the child's care and family environment is residential or boarding education. This is an enormously complex area. Concepts of care and education become almost completely blurred, along with the question of responsibilities between social services and education departments. However, there are many issues here which need to be addressed if special educational needs are to be increasingly met within mainstream education. Residential special schools have a long history. Originally, they were used to provide for children with 'low incidence disabilities' such as blindness and deafness. Here, the rationale for boarding education was relatively clear. It was considered to be educationally impractical to make local provision for such handicaps. However, once residential education emerged as a response to alleviating family difficulties, the educational rationale became less clear. Where, for instance, do the respective responsibilities of social services and education departments begin and end in this area? Questions such as this still reverberate around many a case conference table where special boarding education is proposed for an individual pupil as a response to family needs. Increasing financial pressures frequently lead to 'disputes' between social workers and education officers as to who should 'pick up the bill' for such provision. There is a considerable additional problem once the need to maintain a policy of non-segregation is introduced into the equation. The interplay between social service departments and education departments is significant in this area. Increasingly, it seems that *there are two principles, both concerned with so-called 'normalization' which are in conflict.* On the one hand, social service departments are usually keen to avoid taking care proceedings. Social workers are likely to want to retain the care and control of children from disadvantaged and troubled backgrounds with the child's natural parents. Where this is seen to require a considerable measure of support from an ordinary school and/or some periods of time where the child is cared for outside of the home environment, there is often a call for a day or residential special school. Special education, and particularly boarding special school, can become a means of avoiding care proceedings on the part of social service departments. However, such a move flies in the face of the attempts within the education service to maintain children with special needs in ordinary schools. From the perspective of educational workers, the removal of a child into an alternative care situation is sometimes seen as the means of avoiding a breakdown in mainstream schooling. Thus, two equally valid principles can stand in opposition to each other. As the policies of social service departments increasingly reflect concepts of community care, the avoidance of institutional placements and the closure of community homes with education, the problems outlined here will be magnified. Special schooling, whether residential or day, can become the expedient sought by social workers to contain troubled, delinquent and handicapped pupils for whom there are inadequate community care facilities. Certainly, for most of the children there is likely to be some kind of educational difficulty to which social workers, or other professionals can point. However, does the responsibility for solving the problem rest with the Education Department or the Social Services Department? The absence of any clarity regarding the educational grounds for residential education further muddies already murky waters.

It is doubtful that there are any children currently placed in boarding/residential schools whose placement could be justified on purely educational grounds. Rationale based upon the need for a consistent 24-hour educational programme is sometimes advanced for children with severe, mental handicaps as well as for those with emotional/behavioural difficulties. However, criteria such as these rarely stand up to close scrutiny. All children require consistency of management and care. This does not imply that all children should live with and be educated by the same people in the same establishment. For some pupils, particularly those who are severely handicapped, there may be a greater need to ensure consistency between carers and teachers. However, this does not amount to a justification for residential education. It implies a need for an *adequate* caring environment, an *adequate* school environment and good *liaison* between the two. Teachers do need to widen the range of their responsibilities for supporting and facilitating the work of parents and care providers. However, they are not parent substitutes. *All children, regardless of the severity of their difficulties, have a right to a home and care environment which is both different and distinct from their school environment.* Residential education serves to confuse these issues. Undeniably it has been, and still is, of enormous benefit to a wide range of youngsters. However, its very existence as something separate to, and different from, a child's care and/or family environment, cannot be justified. The concept of residential special education now needs to be seriously questioned. As it operates at the moment it can undermine the aim of developing policies of non-segregation.

To some extent the problems surrounding residential special education result from the organization of, and managerial separation of, social service and education departments. Arguably, the residential facilities which currently exist within special schools should be jointly managed by social services and education departments. This may be an interim step towards total management responsibility being invested with social services. However, the ultimate aim is for children to be able to attend a mainstream school *and* to retain a firm link with their own parents/legal guardians and home. Neither segregated special education nor removal into alternative care is desirable. If the movements towards community care and non-segregated education are to be realized, then the development of more flexible local authority provision is required. Jointly managed and jointly resourced residential hostels may offer an alternative for both disadvantaged and handicapped pupils. Hostels, based in the local community, would offer children whose 'home circumstances were prejudicial to their educational development', some relief from troubled circumstances, without removal into care. At the same time they could continue their education in a mainstream setting. For children with serious mental, physical and sensory handicaps hostels could offer relief to parents on a flexible basis, while parents would retain their overall responsibilty for the child. For this group too, such facilities could meet a wide range of special needs without prejudicing their right of access to education within a mainstream school environment.

Comment

This chapter has looked at the interaction between special educational needs, home background and the needs and wishes of parents. As with many issues in special education a paradox emerges. On the one hand, parents of children with special needs are playing an increasingly positive role in determining the nature and location of their child's education. In contrast, we need to recognize the extent to which parents themselves often have considerable, and extensive, special needs. An interactive notion of special educational needs implies that the educational problems of some pupils are engendered, or at least magnified, by parental and home background factors. Special education is then regarded as a response to such needs.

A number of implications have been identified in this chapter. Firstly, it has been suggested that, in the main, residential special schools should be replaced by community-based facilities, which would permit children to have continued access to both mainstream schooling and to their home/care environment. Secondly, it has been stressed that ordinary schools and ordinary teachers need to be able to assume greater responsibility for links with the parents and homes of children with special needs. This is a characteristic of many good special schools and much can be learnt from their activities in this area. The resourcing of ordinary schools to meet special educational needs should take very clearly into account this area of increased responsibility. Nowhere is this need more apparent than within mainstream secondary schools. Here, the suggestion that teachers might be involved in visiting the homes of pupils, especially those with a range of social behavioural difficulties, is sometimes greeted with surprise and alarm. Yet, the 'received wisdom' of many ordinary school teachers is that childrens' special needs result from parental and home background factors. Meeting special educational needs must therefore involve schools in making a response to factors which stretch well outside the four walls of the school classroom.

Chapter 10

Summary and Conclusions — Making the Ordinary School Special

Currently our concept of a normal school is that of a place into which 'special' children can be integrated or, alternatively, a place from which they can be segregated. However, concepts of 'normality' in education can be altered and broadened by the implementation of policies which are focussed upon non-segregation. Non-segregation policies are central to the theme of 'making the ordinary school special'. By becoming 'special', ordinary primary and secondary schools can become more fully comprehensive in meeting the range of needs which exist in the communities which they serve. In the process, the distinction between 'special' and 'normal' becomes blurred and, ultimately, may have little meaning. Some of the processes involved in bringing about this transition have formed the substance of this book. This chapter provides a summary of some of the major issues involved.

Positive Discrimination for Children with Special Needs

At the heart of non-segregation policies is the principle of *positive discrimination*. As moves are made to merge special education with mainstream education, the importance of the principle of positive discrimination increases. Too often, meeting special needs is seen as being simply a matter of resources. Resource policies constitute an important part, but only a part, of the positive discrimination principle. Adequate resourcing alone does not guarantee that children with special educational needs will have their needs met, nor that they will be accepted and valued within mainstream education. Teachers in separate special schools will often argue that 'their' children will not receive a good deal if they are integrated into the mainstream. Views of this kind are essentially expressions of doubt as to whether positive discrimination will be able to operate for vulnerable, handicapped and disadvantaged children, other than in a separate system. The concern is not exclusively with the distribution of teaching resources, but also with less tangible aspects of positive discrimination. Thus, the meaning of positive discrimination for children with special educational needs must be carefully unravelled as part of any policy leading to non-segregation or integration. Positive discrimination is closely linked to the ideas of equality of right and equality of purpose for children with special needs. Notions of equality for children with special needs rest upon the principle expressed in the Warnock Report that, 'The purpose of education for all children is the same; the goals are the same'. Warnock stated two major goals of education which were seen as common to all: increased knowledge and understanding and progress towards independence. Children with special needs thus have an equal right to the opportunities offered by education. Handicaps, special needs and disabilities are viewed as obstacles towards realization of these goals — obstacles requiring some compensation — hence special education. Special education is a recognition of the need for something additional, something extra to that received by everyone else. The 'something extra' acts to compensate for the obstacles engendered by handicaps and disabilities, which might hinder an individual child's progress towards common educational goals. Severely and multiply handicapped children are working towards the educational goal of independence just as much as their able-bodied peers. They will be on a very different rung of the ladder leading towards independence. They will usually be seen as both requiring and deserving appreciably more input of teacher time, equipment and financial resources than their normal peers, to achieve the next step towards personal independence. Recognition and acceptance of this ethical point is the bedrock of the positive discrimination principle. It is a recognition that some children, because of the obstacles and barriers which confront them, should receive more help than others. The 'something more' might mean more resources, more time, or more consideration. Positive discrimination for children with special needs does not imply that they are more highly regarded or valued than their 'non-special' peers. It implies equal worth and equal regard. Yet such equality is only achieved when exceptional measures are taken on behalf of those with special needs. Positive discrimination does not necessarily imply that children receive something different. One aspect of positive discrimination for children with special needs is that in some respects they are treated equally rather than differently. For pupils who demonstrate severe behavioural difficulties to be equally valued and regarded by their teachers is in itself an aspect of positive discrimination. They are being equally valued in spite of the obvious difficulties which they pose for teaching staff.

Positive discrimination for children with special needs has always existed. Historically, it has existed largely, but not solely, within separate special schools and units. A separate special education system comprising not only special school teachers but administrators, special advisers and professional groups such as educational psychologists, has grown up to serve and expand this positive discrimination system for children with special needs. Arguably, the very separation of this system from mainstream education has effectively prevented the realization of the positive discrimination principle. Sometimes it would appear that the reverse is true — that separation provides a stigmatized, negative discrimination system. This is seen most clearly in the case of children from ethnic minority groups. Negative feelings are frequently expressed by the parents of children from ethnic minority groups when special educational provision is recommended, for example, parents of Afro-Caribbean children in the ILEA (ILEA, 1985a). Special school or special unit placement is not always regarded by such groups as helpful and desirable, but rather as a form of negative discrimination. The important point is that positive discrimination for children with special needs has developed largely in isolation from mainstream education. Remedial education has certainly existed in the mainstream sector. As such, remedial education is an aspect of the positive discrimination principle operating within the mainstream. However, remedial education has traditionally been the 'Cinderella' area of mainstream primary and secondary education. It has often been the first area to be cut during any period of financial difficulties. Moreover, it has not been regarded historically as a high profile, high status aspect of the education service. Separate segregated special education has provided the clearest area for positive discrimination in terms of the allocation of resources for children with special needs. It has also been the area which offered positive discrimination to teaching and professional staff in terms of promotion prospects, salary and career development. *Separate special education has largely prevented the principle of positive discrimination from even being regarded as an issue for discussion within mainstream education.* Instead, the mainstream system has been able to be dominated by 'market forces' in deciding such things as priorities for resource distribution, the status and career development of teachers, the nature of the school curriculum, etc. For an individual mainstream school to declare, and implement, a unilateral policy of positive discrimination towards children who are educationally disadvantaged, would require considerable courage and fortitude. Such a policy could well be seen as disadvantageous to other so-called 'normal' children. The most able and 'future wealth providers' might be seen to suffer as a consequence. In effect, the market forces which operate, particularly upon mainstream secondary schools, lead to a form of positive discrimination not for the least advantaged but for the most advantaged. Special education is there to look after the casualties.

The major challenge for the implementation of non-segregation policies lies in the development of the positive discrimination principle towards children with special needs in ordinary schools. For such a principle to be effective implies significant changes in terms of policy and practices both at the level of individual schools and at the level of the LEA.

Positive discrimination is essentially an ethical matter. Like all ethical issues it is also essentially political. It relates to questions of human values and personal attitudes. Whether positive discrimination for children with special needs should be a principle underlying policy at the level of schools or the LEA cannot be decided by appeal to evidence or scientific research. It is a question of what *ought* to be rather than whether or not something works.

Positive Discrimination — LEA Policies

Positive discrimination will require policies in which children with special needs are accorded *equal value* as individuals alongside their non-special peers. To value equally a child who is less successful, learns more slowly and requires more work and personal input from teachers, is itself an expression of positive discrimination. How can such values be expressed by LEAs and schools? It is not possible to legislate for human values and attitudes, but the way in which society distributes and disperses its resources, and the way in which it confers status and rewards on its members, have an enormous impact on the values and attitudes of individuals. It is these aspects which can be directed and controlled by decisions of policy.

If non-segregation policies are to be pursued by an LEA, then positive discrimination as a principle needs to be explicitly stated by an authority. It will then need to be reflected in all aspects of LEA policy which relate to children with special needs. (There will be few policies, if any, which do not so relate.) *Resource policies* which confer positive discrimination upon children with special needs are likely to be an essential aspect. Favourable teacher/pupil ratios and favourable levels of financing have always been a feature of separate special education. However, to achieve positive discrimination of this kind has always relied upon the ascertainment and processing, and more recently, the 'statementing' of individual children as part of the ritual for legitimizing such discrimination. It has left open the question of whether we are effectivly conferring something positive on the children concerned, or whether we are subjecting them to a form of segregation and stigmatization. For positive discrimination to operate across the *whole continuum of special need*, and as part of mainstream schooling, requires a somewhat different approach. Resource policies will need to focus upon *'increasing what is normally available'* within mainstream education to meet previously unmet needs. A special need only becomes special insofar as it is not 'normally met'. The thrust of LEA policy should be towards *general* as opposed to individual resource strategies. General resource policies which confer positive discrimination, and distribution of available resources towards children with special needs, would need to be made clear and explicit. Several LEAs have evolved methods of resourcing schools which have involved enhanced resourcing because of special educational needs. Headteachers and their schools can be blissfully unaware of this. All resources are treated as one by schools and the positive discrimination aspect may be lost. Such schools may then look outside of themselves to an alternative and separate resource system as a response to meeting children's special needs. Teachers, headteachers and the governing bodies of ordinary schools need to be able to 'see' the additional resources made available to them for children with special needs. This does not imply the separation of special teachers or facilities. Rather, it requires LEAs to continue to make *evident* and *explicit* the way in which they are resourcing schools in terms of positive discrimination measures and, in turn, make clear what is *expected* of schools in terms of meeting special educational needs.

'Whole school'/general resource policies which are linked to a positive discrimination principle will have a number of effects. They should reduce to a minimum the need for procedures which require individuals to be assessed for their 'resourceworthiness'. 'Statementing', under the 1981 Act, operates in part at least, as an institutionalized ritual for limiting and deciding upon the resourceworthiness of individual children. Statements are seen as offering 'protection' to the children concerned. But, from whom are the children being protected? Could it be that the children are being protected from the same

LEAs whose responsibility it is to ensure they receive appropriate education?! Protection is only an issue in the field of special education because the aims, purposes and values of the educational system are not clearly aligned with meeting the individual needs of children. Within a policy framework which has positive discrimination writ large, the need for individual resource procedures, such as statements, will be greatly reduced. They will only be required to meet exceptional needs which (a) could not have been predicted at the level of an individual school or group of schools; and (b) require a highly specific form of resourcing to meet unique needs. As the requirement for the individual 'needs-testing' of children is reduced, so will the requirement for certain professional groups to act as 'gatekeepers' and 'definers of resourceworthiness'. The development of whole school special needs resource policies, linked to the positive discrimination principle, can obviate the need for groups such as educational psychologists to engage in largely irrelevant 'assessment' work. Resources can then be switched into ordinary schools rather than being used to increase the ranks of those operating externally. Instead, provision can be kept 'close to where the action is' — within ordinary classrooms. A new and potentially exciting prospect opens up for 'support' staff personnel. Their work can become more closely linked to intervention, alongside teachers, with children who have serious educational difficulties. Intervention, rather than 'defining', becomes the focus of their work. In addition, their monitoring and evaluation role within the LEA assumes a new and vital importance.

Resource policies are but one element of positive discrimination measures. The *quality, status and career development of teachers* involved in meeting special needs are equally important aspects. Positive discrimination needs to be clearly evident in an *LEA's staffing and recruitment policies*. The absence of positive discrimination outside of separate special schools has meant that able, competent and ambitious teachers seeking career advancement have either had to work within a special school, or have had to avoid the area of special educational needs. A minority has remained in mainstream education and received appropriate recognition in terms of status and salary. Two questions can be regarded as 'acid tests' of the positive discrimination principle in this area:

1 How many headteachers of mainstream comprehensive schools have had substantial previous experience of working with children with special educational needs?

2 How many senior management staff in schools would advise

talented and ambitious young teachers to gain substantial
perience of working in the field of special education as
important part of their career progression?

The implementation of non–segregation policies would be
greatly enhanced by reflecting positive discrimination in staff recruitment and career development practices. Consider, for example, the
implication of each and every senior appointment in an LEA —
ranging from administrators, advisers, headteachers, deputy heads and
other senior staff — having as a prerequisite that candidates could
demonstrate substantial and successful previous experience in meeting
a wide range of special educational needs. Procedures of this kind
contrast sharply with the present realities of staff recruitment and
career development. Currently the chances are remote that someone
with extensive experience of meeting special educational needs would
be seen as a viable candidate for a senior management post in mainstream education. If this situation was reversed, meeting special
educational needs would increasingly be seen as central rather than
peripheral to the way in which mainstream schools operate. Positive
discrimination in this area would have automatic consequences in the
field of in-service training. Training staff to meet special needs would
be high on the agenda of all authorities for all teachers. Training
would not, as is the case now, depend upon government intervention
to make it an area of national priority.

Positive discrimination towards children with special needs
would be reflected in other areas — such as the building of schools.
The needs of handicapped and disabled children would become a first
consideration rather than, as is sometimes the case, an afterthought —
something to be added if finance allows. Lifts, ramps and suitable
hygiene arrangements for disabled children would be built in, as a
matter of course. They would become part of what is 'normally
available'. Similarly, LEA policies relating to curriculum development, and particularly the new curriculum initiatives which are occurring, would be affected in many important respects. A first consideration for any LEA would be the extent to which curriculum development *included* children with special needs. Curriculum initiatives such
as TVEI would automatically need to include all pupils presently
regarded as 'special' — whether they were educated inside or outside
of mainstream schools.

A final, but important, aspect of positive discrimination at the
LEA level relates to aspects of *monitoring*. There are three areas in
which monitoring is of concern. The first relates to the gathering of

information and data on the needs of pupils in schools as part of a resourcing model. A number of authorities have, in either an embryonic, or well developed form (for example, ILEA), established research and statistics departments as part of their organization. Structures of this kind can facilitate the gathering of information about the population, and about the needs of the community being served. The numbers of pupils who come, for example, from under-privileged or disadvantaged backgrounds, who lack fluency in English, who qualify for free school meals or come from large families, would be the sort of data which, once gathered, could inform an LEA's resourcing policies. Secondly, LEAs will need to monitor the extent to which positive discrimination as a principle operates and is maintained over time. Here the concern is to ensure that the resources earmarked for children with special needs are effectively attributed to them. In this area the work of support service personnel acting as the 'eyes and the ears' of the LEA will be important. The third and more controversial area of monitoring relates to the monitoring of pupil performance and the performance of schools. LEAs will need to both ask and answer the question — *what information needs to be gathered about pupil performance, and the performance of schools, as part of a principle of positive discrimination?* The information routinely gathered about pupil performance reflects the values held about the aims and purposes of schools. There is little available information relating to the kind of information which is currently routinely collected by LEAs. However, it is likely that authority-wide screening procedures, based upon pupil attainment levels in basic skill areas, predominate at the primary stage. At the secondary level, success in public examinations usually becomes the focal point of both LEA and public monitoring. If the monitoring of both pupils and schools is based *only* upon 'success' criteria of this kind, positive discrimination for children with special needs will remain a pipe dream. We need to ask whether the same criteria would be seen as relevant for monitoring and appraising special schools for children with severe mental handicaps? Meeting the full continuum of needs within mainstream education must raise all the important questions in education about what constitutes success for both pupils and schools. What are the aims of education? Our notions of educational success, of what is educationally relevant and worthwhile for children, must be redefined. These are essentially ethical, moral and political issues. However, whatever the implications of this process of redefinition, it seems clear that alternative methods of both LEA and in-school monitoring will be required. Alternative forms of monitoring would need to place considerably less emphasis on assessing and comparing pupils against some kind of norm or average expectation. What sense could it make to ask how well a multiply handicapped child is doing in terms of reading skills as set against the norm for his/her age group? Similarly, what sense could it make to compare schools attempting to meet widely varying levels of need, against the single criterion of examination success? For a significant number of pupils, examination success has not, and will never, constitute a valid educational aim. Monitoring children with special needs against such a yardstick is analagous to assessing the performance of wheelchair-bound pupils in terms of their ability to complete a 100 metre run!

Within a non-segregated system the performance of pupils and the performance of schools will need to be judged firstly against increasingly more *differentiated* criteria of progress and success. Secondly, pupil and school performance can only ever be appraised *relative* to particular starting points. We do not expect a physically handicapped child to run as fast, or as far, as an able-bodied child. For such an individual we need to question both their comparison against a norm and the relevance of 'running' as a goal. While the aims of education may be the same for all children, the selection of relevant goals differs significantly between individuals who have widely different starting points. We monitor desired educational outcomes. Educational outcomes will depend upon an individual's particular starting point, in terms of current skills and knowledge, levels of independence, capacity for enjoyment, etc. Progress and success are relative matters. Monitoring an individual's progress over time must therefore involve monitoring educational outcomes judged against their *reasonableness and relevance for a particular individual child*. Traditional methods of monitoring pupil progress in terms of comparative/normative measures have fudged the educational issues involved. They represent a futile search for objectivity and provide simple and incomplete responses to complex questions. The fact that success can only be judged with reference to a child's starting point suggests that authority-wide monitoring is probably not feasible. Statistics relating to matters such as pupil attendence, levels of truancy, suspensions and levels of disruptive behaviour can certainly be collected. They have as much (or as little) validity as do measures of pupil attainment and examination success. They may indeed provide some indicators of the extent to which schools are meeting pupils' needs. However, it is quite possible for a school to have a 100 per cent attendance record, no disruptive behaviour, but to be doing nothing educationally worthwhile for its pupils. What is educationally worthwhile? What constitutes a relevant educational goal for a pupil? How do we gauge the extent to which pupils are progressing? These are questions which can only be answered for an individual pupil by all those who have a concern for that individual's educational and personal welfare.

The Search for Similarities

The search for similarities is the second major principle which underpins non-segregation policies. Developing such policies involves a commitment from educators to *search for similarities as a method of meeting diverse needs*. Herein lies one of the many paradoxes of special education. Segregated special education is the result of processes in which the differences, which so obviously exist between children, are emphasized. As a result of these 'differences', children with special needs are placed in *different* schools where they are taught by *different* teachers, and where *different* personnel (advisers, administrators, HMI) support and administer a *different* system of education. This process of searching for differences has, over the years, become a highly specialized one. Categories of handicap and disability have enhanced the process of looking for differences. Thus, there has been a concern to find a discrete form of special educational treatment linked to ever more refined diagnostic categories of handicap and disability.

If non-segregation policies are to be effective these processes need to be reversed. What is required instead is a conscious search for similarities. A search for similarities between children with diverse needs, between teachers with diverse backgrounds and experiences and between administrators, advisers and support service personnel, despite their differing responsibilities and concerns. This search for similarities does not involve any negation of the need for a so-called differentiated curriculum, a curriculum matched to pupil needs. Nor does it involve any down-grading of the skills and expertise of specialists — whether in the field of special needs or otherwise. Rather, it represents an important point of emphasis when more integrated systems and ways of working are desired.

Similarities Amongst Children

All children are different from one another, but at the same time have similar needs, desires, interests and aspirations. There is not one group of children who are special while the remainder are normal. There is a need to emphasize the similarities rather than the differences between those children regarded as special and those not so regarded. Similarly, where a need is perceived for particular special educational provision (for example, special unit, designated school, etc.), such provision should encompass a broad range of needs rather than some specific category of 'special child'. Thus *generic*, rather than specific, and discrete forms of provision need to be developed. The same view might be taken of existing special schools, i.e., that they should encompass a broad range of needs rather than a discrete handicapped group. Arguably the idea of a special school makes little sense within a comprehensive educational system. It certainly seems to defy any logic to have on the one hand the ideal of a fully comprehensive school, and on the other hand a special school which is highly special-ized, discrete and selective in terms of the client group served. If selective education is a good thing for children with special needs then why is it not a good thing for all — including children within comprehensive, non-selective, primary and secondary schools?

Similarities Amongst Teachers

All teachers are different. They have different expertise, different experiences, different priorities and different interests. Yet all teachers are similar in important respects, and it is these similarities which need to be emphasized. All teachers would want to be seen as having a concern for children and for children's welfare. All teachers are concerned with responding to individuals and individual needs. All teachers would express a concern to maximize the potential progress of pupils in their care. All teachers have expertise in facilitating and optimizing learning. These similarities are the bedrock of what it means to be a teacher of children — whether the children concerned are 'A' level candidates or those with severe mental handicaps. All teachers are teachers of children with special needs. Helping all teachers to become better teachers of children with special needs must begin with a recognition of their existing strengths, skills and competences, rather than their lack of 'special expertise'. Emphasis needs to be placed upon the similarities between 'special teachers' and mainstream teachers rather than upon their differences. Support-ing mainstream teachers to meet special needs must involve *increasing their opportunities* to develop and employ their existing teaching skills with an increasingly diverse range of pupils. This must involve a resource system which enables mainstream teachers to devote more time to individualizing their approach to children with special needs, as well as increasing their opportunities for receiving training and advice. The barriers which exist between mainstream and 'special' teachers need to be minimized. The payment of 's' allowances to special teachers is one such barrier. While such payments may have had a historical rationale they are now an absurdity and needs to be scrapped. Another significant barrier is the mythology of a separate exclusive form of teaching expertise — possessed by special educators but not by their mainstream colleagues. Special education support services and those responsible for the training of teachers need to work towards dispelling this myth. Ultimately, it will disappear as a result of increasing the proximity between special education and mainstream education. *Cooperative working* between remedial/special educators and their mainstream colleagues will demonstrate that both groups have the potential to develop and enhance each other's skills in meeting a more diverse range of needs.

Similarities Beyond the School

Beyond the school we have administrators, advisers, inspectors, psychologists, HMIs and those responsible for teacher training. The search for similarities here will have considerable implications in terms of roles and functions.

The search for a 'whole authority' approach to special educational needs will involve a search for similarities between special administrators, special advisers and their mainstream counterparts. In the same way that the idea of exclusive and specific expertise has evolved amongst teachers in the field of special education, it has also evolved at the level of officers within the LEA. Thus, the AEO (Special Education) and the Adviser (Special Education) can be seen as fulfilling distinctive and exclusive roles with little or no overlap with their mainstream subject/phase colleagues. Within university departments and colleges of higher education, lecturers and tutors with a special needs brief can operate quite separately from curriculum and phase specialists. Yet, of course, special education is neither a phase of education nor a curriculum area. It is a process which runs across all phases and across all subjects. Meeting special needs is thus a matter not only for all teachers, but for all advisers, all administrators and all concerned with teacher training. The search for similarities in these areas between the 'special' and the 'normal' will involve the progressive devolution and dispersal of special educational responsibilities. Many professionals involved in special education will express the view that their ultimate aim is 'to do themselves out of a job'. At first sight such an aim seems somewhat nihilistic, and although it may never be fully realized in practice it is an appropriate aim, and essential to the development of non-segregation policies. Such an aim is incompatible with increasing the ranks of those working exclusively in the area of special needs. It is incompatible with increasing the territory and domain of the special educators. It is incompatible with increasing the number of individuals involved in defining and assessing individual pupils as being in some way special and separate from their peers.

The search for similarities needs to involve an integrated approach to special needs at the level of LEA administration, LEA advisory services and in the field of teacher training. It must involve broadening the role of those currently working exclusively in the mainstream, to include special educational needs. It must also involve broadening the roles of those involved exclusively in special education, to encompass mainstream responsibilities. Progress towards non-segregation policies within LEAs, and elsewhere, could be judged by the extent to which these processes are occurring.

The principle of searching for similarities is closely related to the issue of the *ownership of responsibility* for children with special needs. Historically, the approach to special education has been one of searching out and emphasizing the differences between the special and the normal. The result has been that personal and professional responsibility for meeting the needs of special children has been increasingly invested in personnel outside of mainstream education. If we ask the question, 'Who, within education, is responsible for children with special needs?', the answer at present is that responsibility is primarily seen to rest with special schools, special units, special education teachers, advisers and administrators with a special educational brief. Special education is owned by these personnel rather than by mainstream schools. The search for similarities between the special and normal would reverse this situation. In this respect, processes in which the ownership of special resources and special personnel passes to the management system of mainstream education, are important. It is unrealistic to expect mainstream headteachers and the staff of ordinary schools to feel personally and professionally *responsible* for children with special needs, when they have little or no influence over the management of resources to meet the children's needs. Of course, the corollary is also true. Ordinary schools cannot expect to receive and manage the necessary resources, without accepting responsibility for the children concerned. In reality, what is likely to be required in the immediate future is a complex system of shared responsibility for both the children concerned and for the management of additional resources. Many ordinary schools are not at the stage of being able to accept full responsibility for all the children in their area. This is particularly the case with pupils whose behaviour is seen as destructive and disruptive — children who 'punish' teachers and other adults who attempt to meet their needs and where no ready-made solution to their problems exists. Nevertheless, in this area too, it is possible over time to monitor progress towards non-segregation. Monitoring would focus upon the extent to which ordinary schools are able to accept responsibility for children with special needs and are themselves enabled by LEAs to have the responsibility for managing special education.

The two principles outlined — positive discrimination and the search for similarities — are fundamental to the development of policies of non-segregation for children with special needs. They represent different sides of the same coin, and indeed there is some tension between them. Positive discrimination implies that some children may be given different treatment from other children. Historically establishing positive discrimination has usually reflected a desire to protect both the children concerned and the resources which they require. 'Protection' has involved the separation and segregation of the children, and of the schools and services responsible for meeting their needs. Many educationalists hold the belief that the initial separation of both special children and special resources is a necessary first step towards later integration. Yet such a process seems peculiarly at odds with the idea of a continuum of need. Where would protection and separation begin and end? Rather than being in conflict with the principle of positive discrimination, the search for similarities is, in fact, one aspect of it. One of the ways in which we positively discriminate in favour of handicapped individuals in our society is by *regarding* them and *responding* to them, in spite of their disabilities and difficulties, in ways that are *similar* to those we adopt with the non-handicapped. The need to protect, and to segregate in order to do it, occurs when there is less than unanimous agreement in society about the principle of positive discrimination.

What Can Be Done Tomorrow? — Training and Flexibility

The development of policies of non-segregation poses an enormous challenge to our present educational system. From current starting points, and within particular LEA and school contexts, the challenge may appear to be insurmountable. Policies of positive discrimination which stretch across the whole continuum of need are likely to meet many barriers — political, economic and organizational. In order that such policies be realized what is essentially required is *commitment* from a range of individuals and organizations. Mark Vaughan and Ann Shearer pinpoint the issue of commitment as being a central lesson to be drawn from the experiences of *Mainstreaming in Massachusetts* (Vaughan and Shearer, 1986).

> All sorts of people in all sorts of places in Massachusetts believe that children and young people with special educational needs have a right to participate as fully as possible in the mainstream of their local educational community — and so in the social life of the wider community as well. The belief has brought a raising of expectations — and that has had its positive results. If the Massachusetts experience shows anything, it shows what can be achieved if the commitment is there.

In a similar way in Great Britain, where successful examples of whole school approaches to meeting special needs exist, commitment is always writ large. In particular, the personal commitment of head-teachers to the ideal of meeting all needs, is usually very evident. But how is such a commitment developed? How are the all-important attitudes of teachers, parents, administrators and professional support staff formed and changed? The answer must be that we really do not know. Attitude change is still largely a mystery, both to psychological science and to our common sense understanding of human behaviour. Not surprisingly, discussions about 'integration' often reach the seemingly 'dead-end' conclusion that — 'It's all about changing people's attitudes'. Currently, within the field of special education, attitude change is usually seen as the aim and focus of in-service training for teachers. Not surprisingly, awareness courses and a variety of in-service training initiatives are currently being aimed at mainstream teachers. *Training* is seen as one of the first steps towards change — it is one of the things we can do 'tomorrow'.

In-service training is an important professional *right* for all those in the education service whose work impinges upon children and schools. It contributes to processes such as attitude formation and change. It must not, however, on its *own*, be seen as providing an effective vehicle for change. Organizational psychologists have, for some time, noted the futility of training the individual in order to bring about effective change within complex organizations (Georgiades and Phillimore, 1975). If training is to alter the attitudes, behaviour and performance of the range of individuals concerned with special needs, it must be linked and interlinked with other processes and developments. Training on its own is not enough. Indeed, there exists the possibility that training courses which increase the awareness of teachers within mainstream education can lead to increasing levels of segregation for children with special needs. If we increase awareness without increasing teachers' opportunities to respond practically to children with special needs, this is a very real danger. One of the most important things that can be done 'tomorrow' is to *link training with an increased opportunity* to respond to children with special needs in mainstream settings. Teachers' attitudes towards children with special needs become markedly more positive as a result of their having an opportunity to work successfully with such pupils (Croll and Moses, 1985). Training is but one part of the special needs jig-saw. Too often it is dealt with in isolation from other parts of the puzzle. Often, mainstream teachers are 'sent-off' to be 'trained' and expected to return as unsupported 'hero innovators' to an unchanged school situation. Training, if linked to an overall resource/support network which bears upon the whole school, can be an effective method of bringing about change and progress. For an LEA too, linking resource inputs to training initiatives has its advantages. No LEA is likely to be in the favoured position of having an adequate level of resources to make an input to all ordinary schools at any given time. Linking resources to particular training initiatives acts to legitimize the release of the (usually small) amounts of available resource.

Training which is interlinked with policy can facilitate the development of non-segregation policies. *Obtaining flexibility* is an equally important interim step towards the same goal. Flexibility needs to operate at all levels in the educational system. It must be one of the hallmarks of an educational system capable of responding to diverse needs. Flexibility is required in terms of finance and resources, professional roles, curriculum and teaching methods. While full-blown non-segregation policies may not be immediately realizable, obtaining flexibility may be one of the things that can be worked towards in the short term. A number of examples can be cited.

Teachers in schools require flexibility in order to develop confidence in their ability to meet special needs. They need time and opportunity to develop relevant organizational and curriculum responses. A number of LEAs facilitate this by flexible systems of teacher secondments in order to enable staff to carry out particular pieces of development work for a school and/or the LEA.

Flexibility is required in order that teachers in existing special schools can experience and develop confidence in working within mainstream schools. One-year or one-term teacher exchange schemes can do much to facilitate this and provide a valuable training experience for mainstream teachers. Facilitating this costs little or nothing to an LEA but can provide a significant support to the development of non-segregation policies.

Flexibility of funding is a crucial area. Rigid barriers do sometimes exist in terms of where money can be spent and on what it can be spent. Budget headings can permit significant expenditure on an out-county special school placement, but not allow expenditure upon less expensive in-house provision. Similarly, money is frequently 'saved', or at least unspent, within special education, although, perhaps no mechanism exists within an LEA to release funds for an alternative development. The implication of all this is that education administrators need to establish procedures and mechanisms which permit flexibility in the use of funds, at the point of service delivery.

Flexibility, in terms of the roles played by particular personnel, is vital. Special education is often an area in which territorial disputes can be rife. Thus, conflicts between different advisory and support staff, such as educational psychologists and advisers are commonplace. Such conflicts can lead to fruitless attempts to specify and delimit roles. In special education, more than in any other area, such specification is usually unhelpful. The very essence of meeting special educational needs is that *all* personnel concerned are involved in broadly similar processes.

If non-segregation and positive discrimination policies are not immediately realizable then there are clearly a range of interim steps which can be taken. Ultimately, however, there are difficult questions to be addressed and difficult decisions to be made. For example, should positive discrimination occur for children with special needs? If so, how will it be realized? What are the implications for resourcing and for the career development of teachers? What are the implications for the ways in which we monitor schools? What does the concept of a 'whole school' approach mean in reality? How can a 'whole authority' approach be realized? It is important for those responsible for developing non-segregational policies to keep these questions and decisions at the forefront of discussions about policy and practices in meeting special needs. It is an area in which major ethical, resource and organizational decisions can be easily fudged. 'Easy' solutions to complex problems can be pounced upon and implemented. 'More awareness courses'; 'more advisers'; 'more educational psychologists'; 'more assessment'; 'more expertise' — are all known examples. In isolation from decisions about broad aims and principles, each of these 'solutions' is likely to lead nowhere. *Keeping the agenda in special education clearly focussed upon the central questions and decisions that need to be addressed may ultimately be the most important thing that can be done tomorrow.*

Concluding Comments

The Potential of Special Education

Moves towards 'mainstreaming' and the 'obsession with integration', have at times gravely affected the morale of teachers and other personnel working within the field of special education. This has been the case particularly within special schools. Special school teachers have felt under threat and to some extent devalued and deskilled. Yet special education is currently emerging as one of most exciting areas in which to be professionally involved in the latter half of the 1980s. The excitement of special education lies in its potential to transform and revolutionize what happens in education for all children. It is in this area that the challenge for those involved in special education lies. Sayer (1981) clearly recognized this potential: 'The Warnock Report has quietly unleashed a revolution which is of much greater consequence to the educational process than all the structural transmogrifications which over the past two decades we have described as comprehensive education.'

The potential of special education, and thus the potential contribution to be made by special educators, can be seen in a number of areas. Children who have exceptional needs, those whose difficulties place them at the extremes of any continuum of need, call for exceptional responses from educationalists. Exceptional pupils do not allow for any complacency in terms of issues such as curriculum relevance. There are no easy answers. We cannot afford to look to exam syllabuses or standard curriculum packages in order to decide what should be on offer to a profoundly handicapped child. Such children call for clear decisions to be made about what it is *worthwhile* to teach, what is *worthwhile* for such a child to know and understand. The same child will find learning difficult. This will call for considerable ingenuity and imagination in terms of teaching methods and the delivery of the curriculum. The responses arrived at, whether in terms of curriculum objectives, teaching methods or educational technology, will invariably carry implications for pupils with less exceptional needs, and perhaps, for all pupils.

Responding to the exceptional needs of an exceptional child is but one area in which can be seen the potential of special education to enhance the education system as a whole. Another lies in the overriding concern in special education for the *individual child*. Special education should be an example par excellence of child-centred education. A concern for the rights and dignity of the individual child regardless of handicaps, disabilities and disadvantage is one of the hallmarks of successful special education. This must be a central concern for all teachers and all pupils. Special education has the potential to enhance the efforts of all ordinary schools to develop child-centred education. The staff and personnel who have historically been at the heart of special education are frequently the individuals who possess the personal qualities, attitudes and skills which are most conducive to effecting positive discrimination for handicapped and disadvantaged pupils. If positive discrimination is to become a reality for children with special needs within mainstream schools, then it is in this context that these attitudes, skills and personal qualities must be brought to bear.

These are but a few of the areas in which the potential of special education can be seen. Ultimately, however, the excitement and potential of special education lies in a concern to take the 'special' out of special education. To make what we now consider special to be normal.

Special Education and Democracy

Special education is ultimately about questions of value. It operates in an ethical, political context. It concerns questions about equality and positive discrimination. It addresses questions to do with how much should be spent on which children in our society? Such questions form the background to much of the decision-making which occurs. Positive discrimination towards handicapped and disadvantaged children may be an acceptable principle for the majority of people in any society. However, important questions still remain. *How much* should we positively discriminate? *How much more* should be spent on additional manpower and teaching resources for handicapped and disadvantaged children, in comparison with their more advantaged peers? These questions cannot simply be decided by the so-called 'powers that be'. They affect all members of the society. They affect us all as individuals. They affect what is on offer to all children including our own. In a democratic society, policy in this area must to some extent be a reflection of *what the majority of people want* — what values they hold and what compromises they are prepared to make. Any monolithic policy, unrelated to what the majority of people want and believe in, can have little real future.

To some extent, meeting special educational needs always has been, and probably always will be, a matter of compromise. Separate special schools represent yesterday's 'compromise' to the questions which all societies face about the needs, the rights and the priority to be given to handicapped and disadvantaged individuals. In the future, mainstream schools are likely to provide the base for a new set of compromises. 'Mainstreaming' will not provide any sort of Utopia. It will pose as many questions and uncertainties as already exist about segregated special education. It will be full of compromises. Like all departures from the status quo, it will attract more evaluation, more scrutiny and probably at least as much criticism as anything it replaces. At times, meeting special needs in mainstream schools will be seen as a failure. This will happen for any of a number of reasons — because vulnerable children are 'picked on'; because of increased teacher stress; loss of specially tailored courses; loss of resources to 'ordinary' children; unsympathetic staff, etc. Basic principles will then be called into question and new, or perhaps even old, compromises will be sought. Within a democratic society the particular compromises reached may, at times, not be to our liking. What is perhaps most important is that we are clear about what the real issues are within the field of special education. This book has been written with two aims in mind. Firstly to provide a particular view about the way policy and practices should proceed. Secondly, and perhaps more importantly, to attempt to clarify the underlying issues which need to be addressed if 'ordinary schools are to become special'.

References

AINSCOW, M. and TWEDDLE, D.A. (1979) *Preventing Classroom Failure: An Objectives Approach,* Chichester, Wiley.

BARTON, L. and TOMLINSON, S. (1981) *Special Education: Policy, Practices and Social Issues,* London, Harper and Row.

BARTON, L. and TOMLINSON, S. (Eds.). (1984) *Special Education and Social Interests,* London, Croom Helm.

BLYTHMAN, M. (1985) 'National initiatives: The Scottish experience' in SAYER, J. and JONES, N. (Eds.) *Teacher Training and Special Educational Needs,* London, Croom Helm.

BOOKBINDER, G. (1984) 'Ambiguities and contradictions in the 1981 Education Act (England and Wales)' in *The New Laws on Special Education,* prepared by SWANN, W., BOOKBINDER, G. and O'HAGAN, F. Special Needs In Education Course Team, Milton Keynes, Open University Press.

BOOTH, T. (1982) *National Perspectives,* Unit E241, No. 10 Special Needs in Education, Milton Keynes, Open University Press.

BOOTH, T. (1983) 'Integrating special education' in BOOTH, T. and POTTS, P. (Eds.) *Integrating Special Education,* Oxford, Blackwell.

BOOTH, T. (1985) 'In-service training at the Open University' in SAYER, J. and JONES, N. (Eds.) *Teacher Training and Special Educational Needs,* London, Croom Helm.

BOOTH, T. and PYM, C. (1982) 'Some aspects of special education in Oxfordshire: Innovation and change' in BOOTH, T. and STATHAM, J. (Eds.) *The Nature of Special Education,* London, Croom Helm.

BRENNAN, W.K. (1982) *Special Education in Mainstream Schools — The Search for Quality,* Stratford-upon-Avon, National Council for Special Education.

BUSHELL, R., MILLER, A. and ROBSON, D. (1982) 'Parents as remedial teachers' *Association of Educational Psychology Journal,* 5, 9.

CAMERON, R.J. (Ed.), (1982) *Working Together: Portage in the U.K.,* Windsor, NFER-Nelson.

CONWAY, J. and HEPWORTH, R. (1985) '*An LEA responds to the Education Act 1981*', paper presented to the British Educational Research Association Conference, Sheffield.

COPE, C. and ANDERSON, E. (1977) *Special Units in Ordinary Schools,* Studies in Education 6, University of London Institute of Education, Windsor, NFER.

CROLL, P. and MOSES, D. (1985) *One in Five — The Assessment and Incidence of Special Educational Needs,* London, Routledge and Kegan Paul.

DALY, B., ADDINGTON, J., KERFOOT, S. and SIGSTON, A. (Eds.), (1985) *Portage: The Importance of Parents,* Windsor, NFER-Nelson.

DAVIS, M. (1984) 'Too special, too soon?' *Special Education Forward Trends,* 11, 3, pp 6–8.

DEPARTMENT OF EDUCATION AND SCIENCE (1967) *Children and their Primary Schools* (The Plowden Report), London, HMSO.

DEPARTMENT OF EDUCATION AND SCIENCE (1973) *Staffing of Special Schools and Classes,* Circular 4/73, London, HMSO.

DEPARTMENT OF EDUCATION AND SCIENCE (1978) *Special Educational Needs* (The Warnock Report), London, HMSO.

DEPARTMENT OF EDUCATION AND SCIENCE (1980) *Special Needs in Education,* London, HMSO.

DEPARTMENT OF EDUCATION AND SCIENCE (1981) *Education Act 1981,* London, HMSO.

DEPARTMENT OF EDUCATION AND SCIENCE (1982) *Educational Statistics in Schools,* London, HMSO.

DEPARTMENT OF EDUCATION AND SCIENCE (1983) *Assessments and Statements of Special Educational Needs,* Circular 1/83, London, DES.

DEPARTMENT OF EDUCATION AND SCIENCE (1985a) *Statistical Bulletin,* 13/85, London, HMSO.

DEPARTMENT OF EDUCATION AND SCIENCE (1985b) *Statistical Bulletin,* 14/85, London, HMSO.

DESSENT, T. (1983) 'Who is responsible for children with special needs?' in BOOTH T. and POTTS P. (Eds.) *Integrating Special Education,* Oxford, Blackwell.

DESSENT, T. (1984a) 'Special schools and the mainstream — The resource stretch', in BOWERS T. (Ed.) *Management and the Special School,* London, Croom Helm.

DESSENT, T. (Ed.), (1984b) *What is Important About Portage?,* Windsor, NFER-Nelson.

EDWARDS, C. (1985) 'On launching a support service' *British Journal of Special Education,* 12, 2, pp 53–4.

FERGUSON, N. and ADAMS, M. (1982) 'Assessing the advantages of team teaching in remedial education', *Remedial Education,* 17, 1.

FISH, J. (1985) *Special Education: The Way Ahead,* Milton Keynes, Open University Press.

GALLOWAY, D. (1985) *Schools, Pupils and Special Educational Needs,* London, Croom Helm.

GALLOWAY, D. and GOODWIN, C. (1979) *Educating Slow-Learning and Maladjusted Children: Integration or Segregation?,* London, Longman.

GEORGIADES, N.J. and PHILLIMORE, L. (1975) 'The myth of the hero innovator and alternative strategies for organizational change', in KIERNAN C. and WOODFORD F. (Eds.), *Behaviour Modification for the Severely Retarded,* Amsterdam, Association Scientific.

GILBERT, C. (1986) 'Reconnecting remedial education: Case study, Whitmore High School', unpublished paper, Whitmore School, Harrow.

GILLHAM, B. (Ed.) (1978) *Reconstructing Educational Psychology*, London, Croom Helm.

GIPPS, C. and GOLDSTEIN, H. (1984) 'Remedial service to special needs support team: Is it more than a change in name?', *Occasional Paper No. 4. Screening and Special Educational Provision in Schools Project*, University of London Institute of Education.

GIPPS, C. and GROSS, H. (1984) 'Local education authority policies in identification and provision for children with special educational needs in ordinary schools', *Occasional Paper No. 3. Screening and Special Educational Provision in Schools Project*, University of London Institute of Education.

GOLBY, M. and GULLIVER, J.R. (1979) 'Whose remedies, whose ills? A critical review of remedial education', *Journal of Curriculum Studies*, 11, 2, p. 137–47.

GOODWIN, C. (1983) 'The contribution of support services to integration policy', in BOOTH T. and POTTS P. (Eds.) *Integrating Special Education*, Oxford, Blackwell.

GROSS, H. and GIPPS, C. (1985) 'Do teachers have special needs too? Teachers' reactions to special needs provision' *Occasional Paper No. 5. Screening and Special Educational Provision in Schools Project*, University of London Institute of Education.

HACKNEY, A. (1985) 'Integration from special to ordinary schools in Oxfordshire', *Educational and Child Psychology*, 2, 3, pp 88–95.

HEGARTY, S. and POCKLINGTON, K. with LUCAS, D. (1981) *Educating Pupils with Special Needs in the Ordinary School*, Windsor, NFER-Nelson.

HEGARTY, S. and POCKLINGTON, K. with LUCAS, D. (1982) *Integration in Action*, Windsor, NFER-Nelson.

HINDS, T. (1982) 'Giving heads and governors control of the purse strings' *Education*, 26 November.

HINSON, M. (1985) 'Teachers' involvement in curriculum change' in SMITH C. (Ed.) *New Directions in Remedial Education*, Lewes, Falmer Press.

HOCKLEY, L. (1985) 'On being a support teacher', *British Journal of Special Education*, 12, 1, pp 27–9.

HODGSON, A., CLUNIES-ROSS, L. and HEGARTY, S. (1984) *Learning Together*, Windsor, NFER-Nelson.

INNER LONDON EDUCATION AUTHORITY (1982) *Educational Priority Indices — A New Perspective*, Research and Statistics Report RS858/82, London, ILEA.

INNER LONDON EDUCATION AUTHORITY (1984a) *Improving Secondary Schools*, ILEA Learning Resources.

INNER LONDON EDUCATION AUTHORITY (1984b) *Survey of Characteristics of Pupils in Special Schools and Units*, Report by Education Officer, Item 3, ILEA 4627, London, ILEA.

INNER LONDON EDUCATION AUTHORITY (ILEA) (1985a) *Educational Opportunities For All?*, Report of the Committee reviewing provision to meet special educational needs (The Fish Report), London, ILEA.

INNER LONDON EDUCATION AUTHORITY (ILEA) (1985b) *Children in Need*, London, ILEA.

JONES, E. (1983) 'Resources for meeting special needs in secondary schools' in BOOTH T. and POTTS P. (Eds.) *Integrating Special Education*, Oxford, Blackwell.

JONES, E. and BERRICK, S. (1985) 'Adopting a resources approach' in SMITH C. (Ed.) *New Directions in Remedial Education*, Lewes, Falmer Press.

JONES, N. (1983) 'The management of integration: The Oxfordshire experience' in BOOTH T. and POTTS P. (Eds.) *Integrating Special Education*, Oxford, Blackwell.

JONES, N. (1985) 'Extending the concept of normality', *Education*, 166, 24.

LEWIS, G. (1984) 'A supportive role at secondary level', *Remedial Education*, 19, 3, pp 7–11.

LINDSAY, G. (1985) Introduction to Conference Proceedings — 'Integration: possibilities, practice and pitfalls', *Educational and Child Psychology*, 2, 3, pp 4–7.

Local Government Act 1966, Section II, London, HMSO.

LUKES, J.R. (1981) 'Finance and policy-making in special education', in SWANN W. (Ed.), *The Practice of Special Education*, Oxford, Basil Blackwell.

LUTON, K.A. (1986) 'Learning by doing', unpublished paper, Banbury School, Oxfordshire.

MARRA, M. (1984) 'Parents of children with moderate learning difficulties', in BOWERS, T. (Ed.) *Management and the Special School*, London, Croom Helm.

MITTLER, P. and MCCONACHIE, H. (Eds.), (1983) *Parents, Professionals and Mentally Handicapped People*, London, Croom Helm.

NATIONAL ASSOCIATION FOR REMEDIAL EDUCATION (1979) *NARE Guidelines No. 2: The Role of Remedial Teachers*, Stafford, NARE.

NATIONAL UNION OF TEACHERS (1984) *Meeting Special Educational Needs in Ordinary Schools*, London, NUT.

NEWELL, P. (1985) 'The children's legal centre', *Educational and Child Psychology*, 2, 3, pp 23–30.

NEWSON, E. and HIPGRAVE, T. (1982) *Getting Through to Your Handicapped Child*, Cambridge, Cambridge University Press.

NORWICH, B. (1983) 'The unique contribution of child psychology services', *Bulletin of the British Psychological Society*, 36, pp 116–9.

POTTS, P. (1983) 'What difference would integration make to the professionals?' in BOOTH T. and POTTS P. (Eds.) *Integrating Special Education*, Oxford, Blackwell.

RAYBOULD, T. and SOLITY, J. (1985) 'Teaching with precision' in SMITH C. (Ed.) *New Directions in Remedial Education*, Lewes, Falmer Press.

REYNOLDS, D. (1976) 'When pupils and teachers refuse a truce: The secondary school and the creation of delinquency', in MUNGHAM G. and PEARSON G. (Eds.) *Working Class Youth Culture*, London, Routledge and Kegan Paul.

REYNOLDS, D. (1982) 'The search for effective schools', *School Organization*, 2, pp 215–37.

RUTTER, M., MAUGHAN, B., MORTIMORE, P., OUSTON, J. and SMITH, A. (1979) *Fifteen Thousand Hours: Secondary Schools and their Effects on Pupils*, London, Open Books.

SAYER, J. (1981) 'Down and up the line to integration', *Education*, 17 July.

SAYER, J. (1983) 'A comprehensive school for all' in BOOTH T. and POTTS P. (Eds.) *Integrating Special Education*, Oxford, Blackwell.

SAYER, J. (1985) *What Future for Secondary Schools?*, Lewes, Falmer Press.

SCOTTISH EDUCATION DEPARTMENT (1978) *The Education of Pupils with Learning Difficulties*, Scotland HMI.

SHAPIRO, H.S. (1980) 'Society, ideology and the reform of special education: a study in the limits of educational change,' *Educational Theory*, 30, (3), pp 211–23.

SMITH, C. (Ed.) (1985) *New Directions in Remedial Education*, Lewes, Falmer Press.

SWANN, W. (1985) 'Is the integration of children with special needs happening?: An analysis of recent statistics of pupils in special schools', *Oxford Review of Education*, 2, 1, pp 3–18.

TIZARD, J., SCHOFIELD, W.N. and HEWISON, J. (1982) 'Collaboration between teachers and parents in assisting children's reading', *British Journal of Educational Psychology*, 52, pp 1–15.

TOMLINSON, S. (1982) *The Sociology of Special Education*, London, Routledge and Kegan Paul.

TOPPING, K.J. and WOLFENDALE, S. (1985) *Parental Involvement in Children's Reading*, London, Croom Helm.

TUTT, N. (1985) 'The unintended consequences of integration', *Educational and Child Psychology*, 2, 3, pp 30–9.

VAUGHAN, M. and SHEARER, A. (1986) *Mainstreaming in Massachusetts*, Centre for Studies on Integration in Education (London) and The Campaign for People with Mental Handicaps (Cambridgeshire).

VISLIE, L. (1978) 'Policies for educational integration and its implications for basic education in Norway' in OECD *Study in Basic Education*, Oslo, OECD.

WATERMAN, C. (1983) 'Getting in on the Act', *Education*, 161, 7, pp 128–30.

WEDELL, K. (1981) 'Concepts of special educational need', *Education Today*, 31, 1, pp 3–9.

WEDELL, K. (1983) 'Some developments in the concepts and practice of special education', *New Horizons Journal of Education*, Hong Kong Teachers' Association, 24, pp 99–108.

WILDLAKE, P. (1985a) 'Beyond the sabre-toothed curriculum' in SMITH, C. (Ed.) *New Directions in Remedial Education*, Lewes, Falmer Press.

WILDLAKE, P. (1985b) 'How should we respond to change', *British Journal of Special Education* 12, 2, pp 50–2.

WOLFENDALE, S. (1983) *Parental Participation in Children's Development and Education*, New York, Gordon and Breach.

WOLFENDALE, S. (1985) 'A review of parental involvement and the place of portage' in DALY B., ADDINGTON J., KERFOOT S., and SIGSTON A. (Eds.) *Portage: The Importance of Parents*, Windsor, NFER-Nelson.

Index